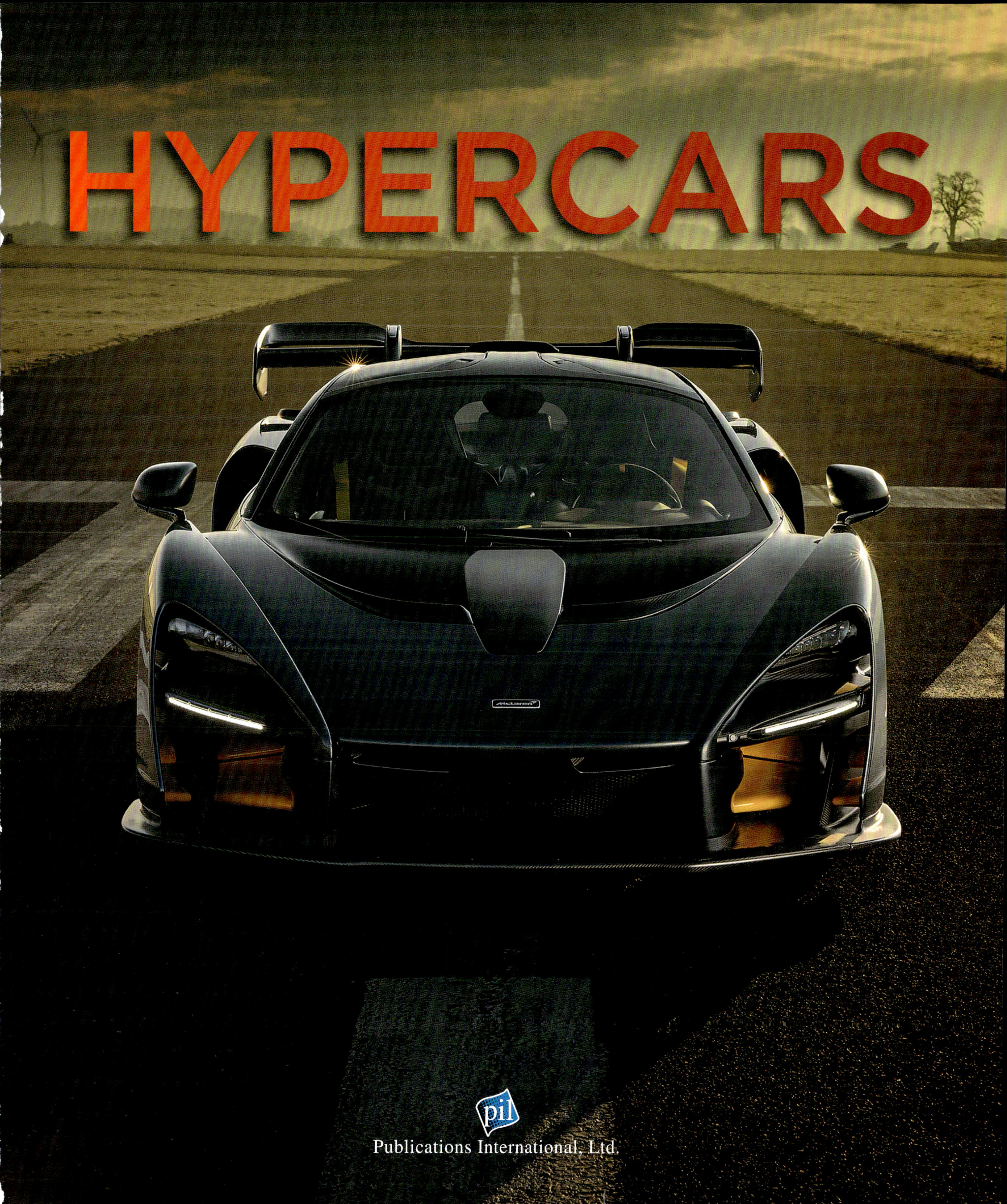
HYPERCARS
pil
Publications International, Ltd.

Special thanks to the following manufacturers who supplied imagery:

Aspark Co., Ltd; Aston Martin Lagonda Limited; Bugatti Automobiles, S.A.S.; Czinger Vehicles Inc.; Daimler AG; De Tomaso Automobili Ltd.; Ferrari S.p.A.; Ford Motor Company; Gordon Murray Automotive; Hennessey Performance; Koenigsegg Automotive AB; Automobili Lamborghini S.p.A.; Group Lotus Limited; McLaren Automotive; NIO Inc.; Noble Automotive Ltd.; Pagani Automobili S.p.A.; Pininfarina S.p.A.; Porsche AG; Rimac Automobili; SSC North America; Stellantis; Ultima Sports Ltd.; W Motors; Zenvo Automotive A/S

Additional images from Shutterstock.com

Louis Weber, CEO
Publications International, Ltd.
8140 Lehigh Avenue
Morton Grove, IL 60053

ISBN: 978-1-63938-924-7

Manufactured in China.

8 7 6 5 4 3 2 1

Table of Contents

Two Seconds

It takes about as long to type those two words as it does for them to pass. It's a speck in time that even the most engaged people are barely aware of. Two seconds, it appears, is what has become the new performance delta for 0–60 miles per hour acceleration. From a dead stop, throttle pinned, the fastest cars in the world are blowing past 60 miles per hour in just two seconds and change. For that matter, in the past several years more and more cars are even achieving sub-two second sprints to 60. It's all happening in what we're now calling the hypercar class. These are the most powerful, best handling, most capable machines money can buy, and they come with dramatic sloping bodies designed to slip through the air while catching the eye of onlookers with their dramatic lines. In the last twenty years, the proliferation of models available in this class has become noteworthy. To the surprise of some, not only does the market exist, but it continues to grow unabated.

In the history of automobiles, there have never been more incredible machines available for purchase. And despite their steep price tags, people are buying them. People cannot seem to get enough of them. The path to the two-second club has never had so many different options.

So yes, those two seconds are an important metric in a book dedicated to hypercars; that's the new rubicon for serious speed. But these hypercars are also demonstrating that 0–60 is no longer the best reliable indicator of a car's real ability. For enthusiasts who grew up checking test results columns of their favorite car magazines, that kind of drag race statistic—just the straight line, no-excuses litmus test—was integral. Times have changed.

With contemporary hypercars breaching 1,000hp regularly and sometimes even knocking on the 2,000hp ceiling, the run to 60 is just one of many metrics. With the power these hypercars have on tap, the question becomes whether the car has stopped spinning its wheels—even *all* wheels—from rest to accelerate at its true maximum.

Even with sophisticated traction aids, all-wheel drive, and semi-automatic transmissions with launch programs designed to find the optimum grip every time, a significant number of the best hypercars are just getting going at 60mph. Perhaps the time it takes to reach 100mph is more telling? Or the time it takes to get through the quarter mile? Has it already given its best at this point? And are the old tests really relevant now? As power increases, the paradigm is shifting. Engineering, aerodynamics, and even the propulsion method now need to be considered.

Method of propulsion, you ask? It's time to address that. In this decade, we have seen ever more power engineered from gasoline engines, but also the increasing use of electric motors and supercapacitors. While some people are skeptical about electric power, the builders and engineers making them are letting the products do the talking. The results speak for themselves. Torque from zero to sky high and electric platforms that allow companies to concoct any kind of design they want with no constraint means the public is starting to see a startling new proliferation of clever designs.

It's important to note how much easier it is to develop a car when using electric motors. Time and again with the hypercars included in this book, we discover that electric motors equate to less development time and less expense. Electric motors are compact and can be put almost anywhere in the car, from the hub to the transmission or anywhere else they can fit. The "skateboard" approach to electric car chassis design (where everything needed to power the car is on a low and flat platform) has significantly reduced the time needed to design, configure, and bring to market new cars. That ease in developing electric-powered models from scratch explains why there are so many players in the hypercar segment relying solely on electric. But that doesn't mean that venerable engine builders have gone extinct. Far from it. There's still a market for big V8s and V12s. For those who prefer the sound and fury of a powerful gasoline engine aided by turbo- or supercharged forced induction, there are still manufacturers dedicated to delivering that experience.

There are also hybrid drivetrain options. These combinations work well enough for Formula 1 and Le Mans racers, so it makes sense that the approach works in fast street cars as well. With electric motors providing power at zero rpms, acceleration becomes smoother. Electric motors also provide extra power out of turns when gasoline engines are low in the rev range and low on power. The combined effort at full throttle makes for incredible power numbers.

Hybrid drivetrains are the most complicated option. They require computers to make everything work harmoniously. Legacy manufacturers, with both the capital and the existing technology already in place, are best positioned to take the hybrid approach to drivetrain production. While hybrid tech may seem an unnecessary compromise to some, the resulting cars use less gas and produce less emissions while still providing the killer soundtrack of a powerful combustion engine and raw boosts of power via electric motors.

While the engineering and technical savvy that goes into hypercar production is stunning, let's not forget to take a moment to just . . . look at them. Whether futuristic or retro, full downforce aero or voluptuous design, just about every style of hypercar is represented in this book. There's no need for restraint in this segment; in the recent past, incredible new shapes and styles have appeared on the market. Turn the page and be prepared to marvel!

Alfa Romeo 33 Stradale

Hypercars specialize in flair, and one of the time-honored ways to stand out is with the doors. The 33 Stradale uses top-hinged "butterfly" doors to heighten the experience.

Alfa Romeo is one of Italy's oldest car companies. It has been at the forefront of making cars with sporting intentions since its inception. This, their latest creation, is the 33 Stradale, a name borrowed from their 1960s sports coupe (18 produced from 1967 to 1969). The 33 Stradale is meant to serve as a through line from their best sporting GTs. Built by the illustrious coachbuilder Carrozzeria Touring Superleggera, this is an exclusive coupe with limited production and a list price of USD $1,000,000.

The development of the 33 Stradale marked Alfa Romeo's intention to return to competition. As an iconic design from Scaglione, it has been singled out as one of Alfa's best-looking cars—no small accomplishment. That status meant that the new version needed to be a formidable machine worthy of the name it carried, both in design and ability.

The new 33 Stradale's design was carried out by Alfa Romeo Centro Stile, with a select team in charge of design and engineering. The result is suitably dramatic and confident, particularly with the oversized rear taillights. The overall shape acknowledges the past while still bringing out modern touches. Overall, it is easy to identify this car as an Alfa Romeo.

Using a chassis from sister company Maserati, the Stradale shares some components with the MC20, including the twin turbo V6. But as a notable difference, Alfa Romeo offers either the TTV6, or a fully electric system developing north of 700hp. This marks the Stradale 33 as the only supercar currently offering the choice to go with either internal combustion or electric propulsion—a status that may best reflect the diverging paths automotive companies are taking at the exclusive end of the automotive market. With only 33 of these scheduled to be produced, the most interesting final statistic may be which type of motor the owners choose for their own hypercar.

Acceleration: est. 0–60mph <3.0 seconds

Power output: 650hp (ICE), 750hp (Electric)

Production years: 2025

Production numbers: 33

Engine: 3.0 liter, twin turbocharged V6, 650hp

Price: est. USD $1,000,000

Minimalist in the classic sense, but with modern capability, the gauge cluster looks old-school analog, but is fully digital with multiple configurations. This customization is achieved without cluttering the interior with buttons. The steering wheel, a simple three-spoke design, has been intentionally left devoid of switchgear.

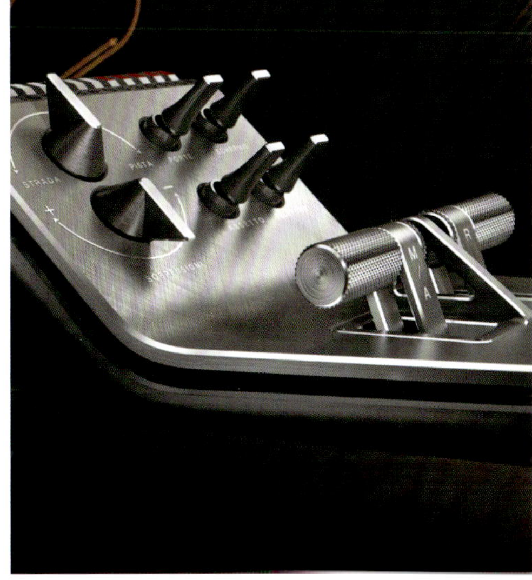

ALFA ROMEO AUTOMOTIVE

One of the oldest automobile manufacturers still in existence, Alfa Romeo has long been an enthusiast's favorite. Remarkably, it has managed to consistently offer memorable machines in almost every category and at almost every price point since its inception in 1910. What established it early on was its sports car offerings. These employed the most advanced technologies, with bodies designed by legendary styling houses from Italy. Models like the 8C from the 1930's were what firmly established Alfa Romeo. These were incredibly successful both as road-going sports cars and in competition—winning races thanks in no small part to Enzo Ferrari's involvement with the company.

Later models like the Spider, Giulia, GTV, and the 1600 sedan brought style and ability to the masses, but Alfa also continued to release incredible limited run coupes. The stunning Marcello Gandini-designed Montreal, the very 1990s SZ or Sprint Zagato, and the more modern 8C and 4C were all eye-catching shapes but always tailored for the driving enthusiast. The new 33 Stradale fits that tradition, but this is a model that belongs in the hypercar segment, with the proper looks and power in either ICE or electric motivation.

Aspark Owl

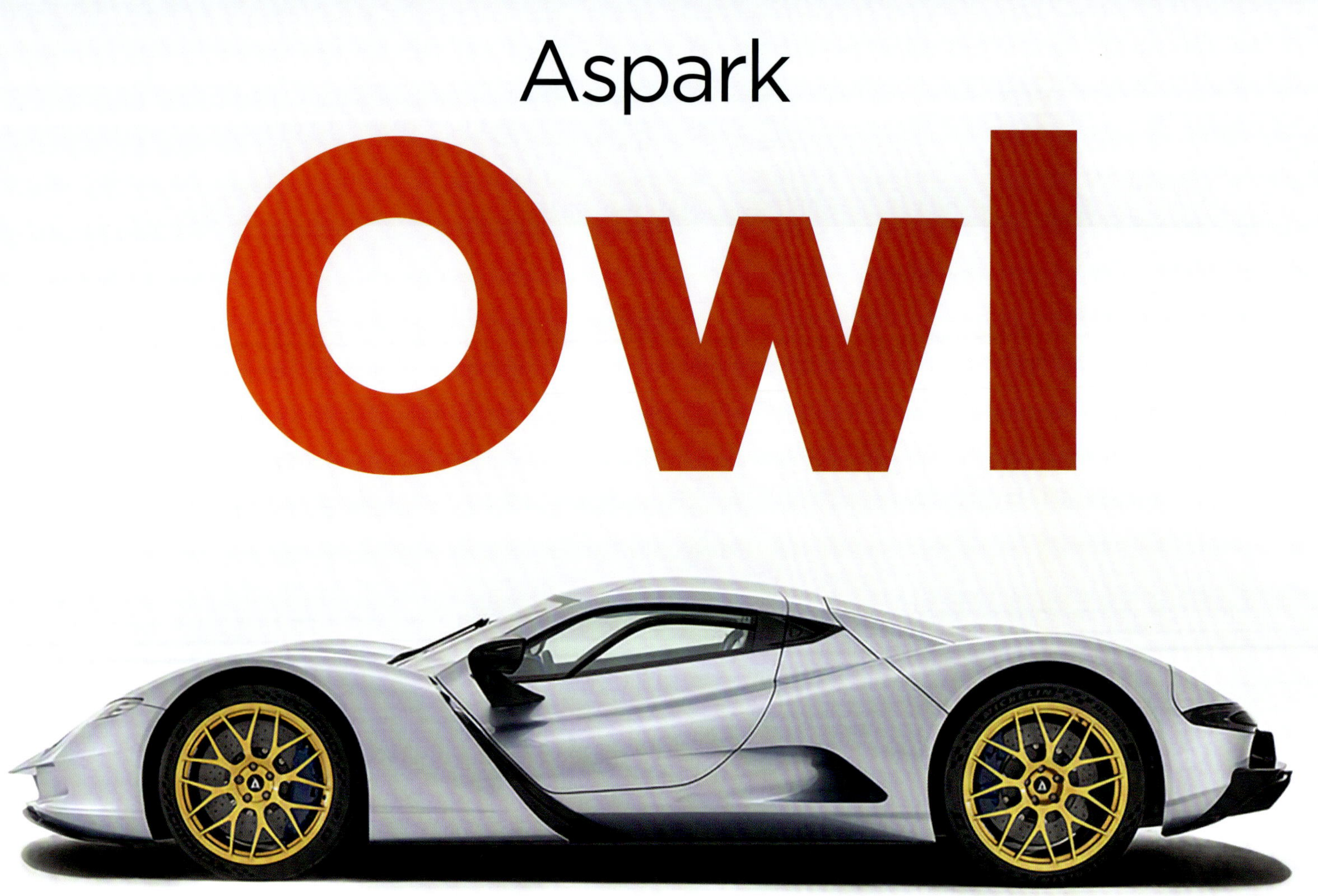

While many businesses have made attempts to enter the hypercar market recently, Aspark has managed to successfully produce a car that not only meets the standards of the hypercar, but sets those standards as well. Aspark sits at the head of the table of the electric hypercar category—the newest and most rapidly developing sector that's bringing jaw-dropping numbers for even the most jaded enthusiast.

When they announced their intention to build the Owl years ago, nobody would have predicted that the upstart would be this successful so quickly. As a company formed in the Osaka prefecture in Japan in 2005, Aspark specialized in engineering and design services for other companies—some in automotive, some in electronics. They designed individual components, but were not responsible for total machine manufacture. So when they announced their intent to build a hypercar in 2015, that deep background helps to explain how they presented their first prototype a mere two years later. They subsequently premiered at the Dubai International Auto Show in 2019 with a functional prototype.

The numbers are suitably breathtaking: 1,953hp, running power through four hub-mounted electric motors at all four wheels, with a carbon-fiber monocoque covered with a notably attractive design. But most impressive is how Aspark developed everything in-house. The model was designed, tested, and engineered by the company and then built by Manifattura Automobili Torino in Italy for the production version, 20 of which are in customer's hands.

A limited production hypercar, as opposed to a mass production car, played to Aspark's strengths. And to make the naysayers hold their tongue, the company asked Guinness Book of World Records to officially record their acceleration tests, ensuring that they were known as the fastest accelerating electric car in the world, through both the 1/8 and 1/4. And when that record was surpassed by Rimac with their Nevera, Aspark took it right back with the Owl N600 in June of 2024.

Aspark can arguably lay claim to the title of first and fastest electric hypercar. Judging by their efforts, they don't plan to give that title up any time soon.

ASPARK AUTOMOTIVE

Based in Osaka, Japan, Aspark began as a supplier and consulting firm for other businesses in 2005. It was one of the myriad firms supporting larger industrial concerns in that country. The origins of the company may seem humble for a hypercar manufacturer at first glance, but providing services for those diverse clients meant that Aspark was learning important lessons about what it took to build their own machine. From engineering to production to software coding and development, the in-house experience and talent development put them in the position to bring their Owl hypercar from concept to production with relative ease.

What's notable in the modern era is how electrification makes it easier for a new company to bring its product to market relatively quickly. Developing an engine and drivetrain for production consumes both time and resources, while buying from an existing manufacturer is no sure thing.

Acceleration: 0–60mph—1.72 seconds

Torque: 1,475 lb-ft

Power output: 1,984bhp

Production years: 2020–2025

Production: 50

Engine: electric, four hub mount motors

Weight: 4,409 lbs

Price: 2.5 million euro

The dihedral doors on the Owl are hypercar-dramatic when opened, but they are functional in their operation. The hinge mechanism allows the door to swing out as it rises up, for easier access to the interior and minimum required contortion for the people lucky enough to sit inside.

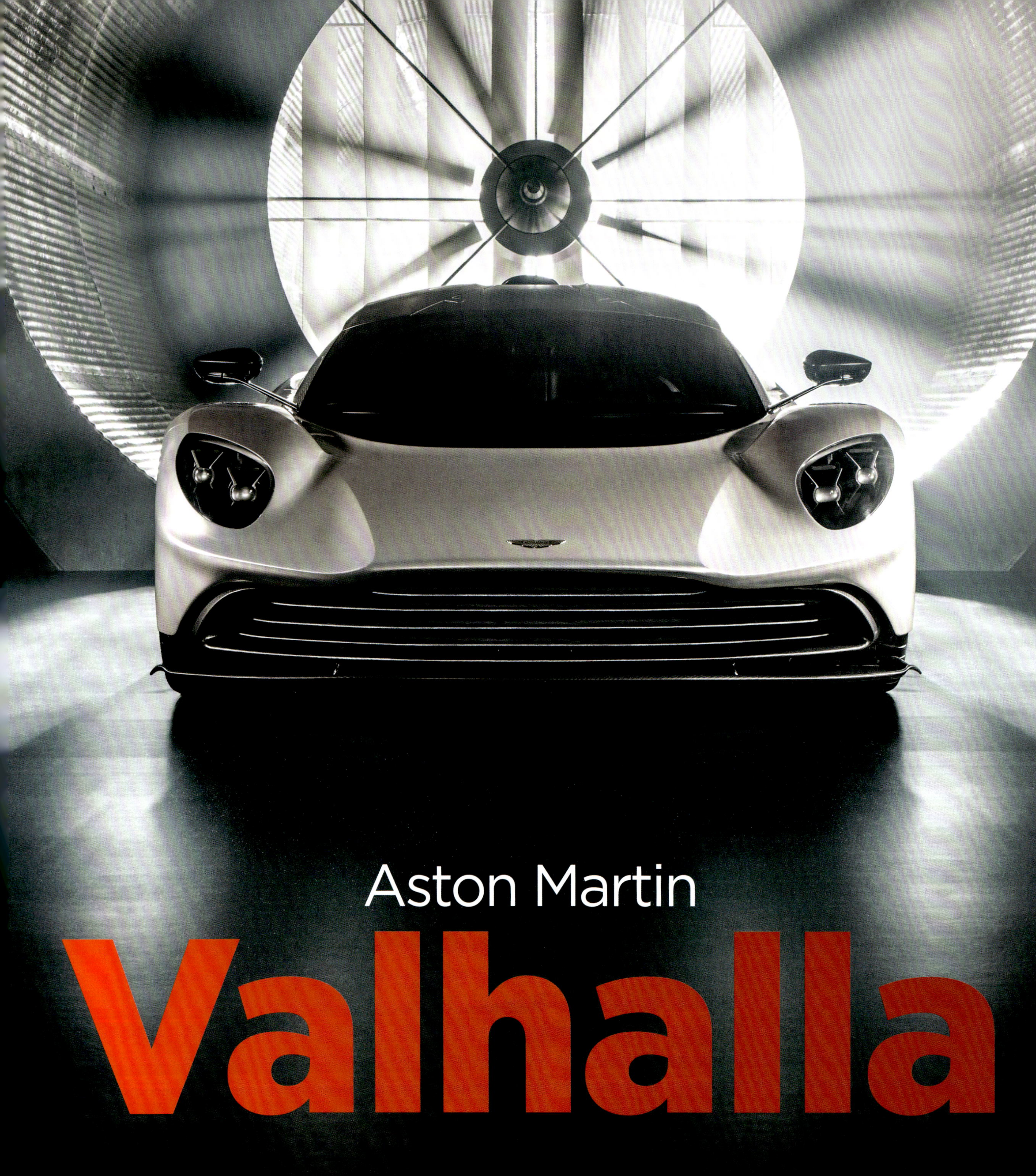

Aston Martin Valhalla

Aston Martin's Valhalla represents the company's belief that, even in the hypercar segment, there is enough room for nuance. The Valhalla's meaner sibling, the Valkyrie, was introduced the year before the Valhalla, and the two hypercars are remarkable for their distinctly different missions. The Valkyrie is a no-excuses, track-oriented bruiser archetype, while the Valhalla focuses on being the smoother, easier GT-oriented character.

Despite being built on a dedicated carbon fiber chassis, the Valhalla is a bespoke unit, with a similar exterior shape to the Valkyrie, but that shares no panels with its cousin. The Valhalla's specifications reveal the smallest of concessions to being "second" to the Valkyrie in performance—a twin turbo flat-plane crank V8 instead of a naturally aspirated V12, and a hybrid drive system that allows electric only propulsion and all-wheel drive instead of rear-wheel drive, along with a dual-clutch, semi-automatic transmission that is much smoother than the single-clutch, sequential unit in the Valkyrie.

With the front-axle drive handled completely by the electric motor, total power output comes to 937 horsepower and 738 lb-ft of torque—down about 200hp from the Valkyrie, yet with slightly more torque. All-wheel drive along with the full complement of driver safety systems like active cruise control, forward collision alerts, and blind spot monitoring means that it promises to be the easier car to pilot than the track-focused special.

The interior of the Valhalla is where the difference between the two models is most apparent. Along with the more spacious size, it features the usual GT amenities like dual zone climate control, and a central touchscreen system with Apple CarPlay and Android Auto connectivity.

Acceleration: 0–60mph 2.5 seconds

Torque: 737 lb-ft

Power output: 937hp

Production years: 2024

Production numbers: 999

Engine: 4.0 liter, twin turbo V8, and front-axle electric motor assist

Weight: 3,400 lbs

Price: est. USD $800,000

Purposeful, but with just enough comfort, the Valhalla is a serious hypercar. Aston Martin decided to tilt the interior's experience towards a seriously rapid GT instead of a barely street-legal track machine.

ASTON MARTIN AUTOMOTIVE

While hypercars are, by definition, the extreme end of the spectrum, Aston Martin enjoys a long history of producing intensely desirable GT road cars. A luxurious version of a hypercar in the Aston Martin idiom makes perfect sense in that context. Gentlemen racers with the discretionary income and ties to Aston Martin racing teams would have the perfect car to arrive at the track in.

Aston found a niche within the hypercar niche—grand touring in tandem with barely tamed race cars—when not everyone was sure buyers would appreciate the distinction. And, like many hypercar projects, drivetrain choices and details changed as the Valhalla got closer to production. Ultimately, Formula 1 tie-ins and race connections made the credible case for Aston Martin. Buyers will likely continue to clamor for these cars.

Aston Martin
Valkyrie

For Aston Martin, the Valkyrie was conceived as a focused, track-oriented machine with only the bare minimum of concessions to driving ease or comfort—as close as you can get to a passion project for a large business. Like many hypercars, it is a halo car; its creators tapped on their experiences in Formula 1 racing to create it. Not merely inspired by former Formula 1 exploits, the Valkyrie is a direct descendant of that race series, as envisioned and brought to fruition by legendary F1 designer Adrian Newey, along with Andy Palmer and Simon Sproule, Aston Martin's CEO and head of marketing, respectively.

The end result is, unsurprisingly, a barely disguised race car. It is decidedly lean and purposeful, looking more like a Le Mans prototype than an exotic street car, with a design shrunken around the cockpit and tightly drawn over the wheels and running gear as closely as possible. No sign of unnecessary flair can be found. Even its interior lacks creature comforts and luxury trimmings, as that would run contrary to the Valkyrie's purpose.

Starting with a carbon fiber tub, Aston adds a naturally aspirated, Cosworth-designed V12 mated with an electric motor that's integrated into the seven-speed, single clutch, sequential gearbox. The Cosworth engine has an 11,100 rpm redline and makes 1,001bhp, while the electric motor brings total power to 1,139bhp; all the power is sent to the rear wheels. The lack of sound-deadening measures in the cabin is emphasized by the presence of two sets of headsets, meant to allow some measure of relief from noise and provide the two occupants a way to communicate. Given the fact that the two passengers would be practically on top of each other, those headsets may be the best evidence of the uncompromising nature of the Valkyrie.

Acceleration: 0–60mph 2.5 seconds

Torque: 663 lb-ft

Power output: 1,160hp

Production years: 2023–2024

Production numbers: 175 (150 street, 25 AMR Pro)

Engine: 6.5 liter V12, with electric motor assistance

Weight: 2,271 lbs

Price: est. USD $3,500,000

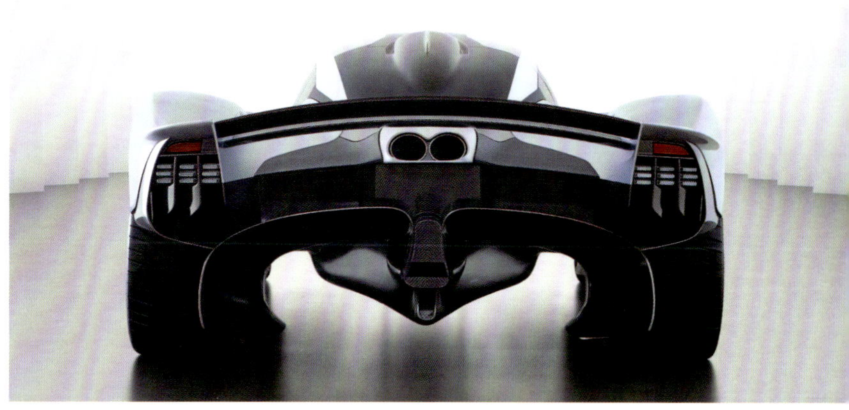

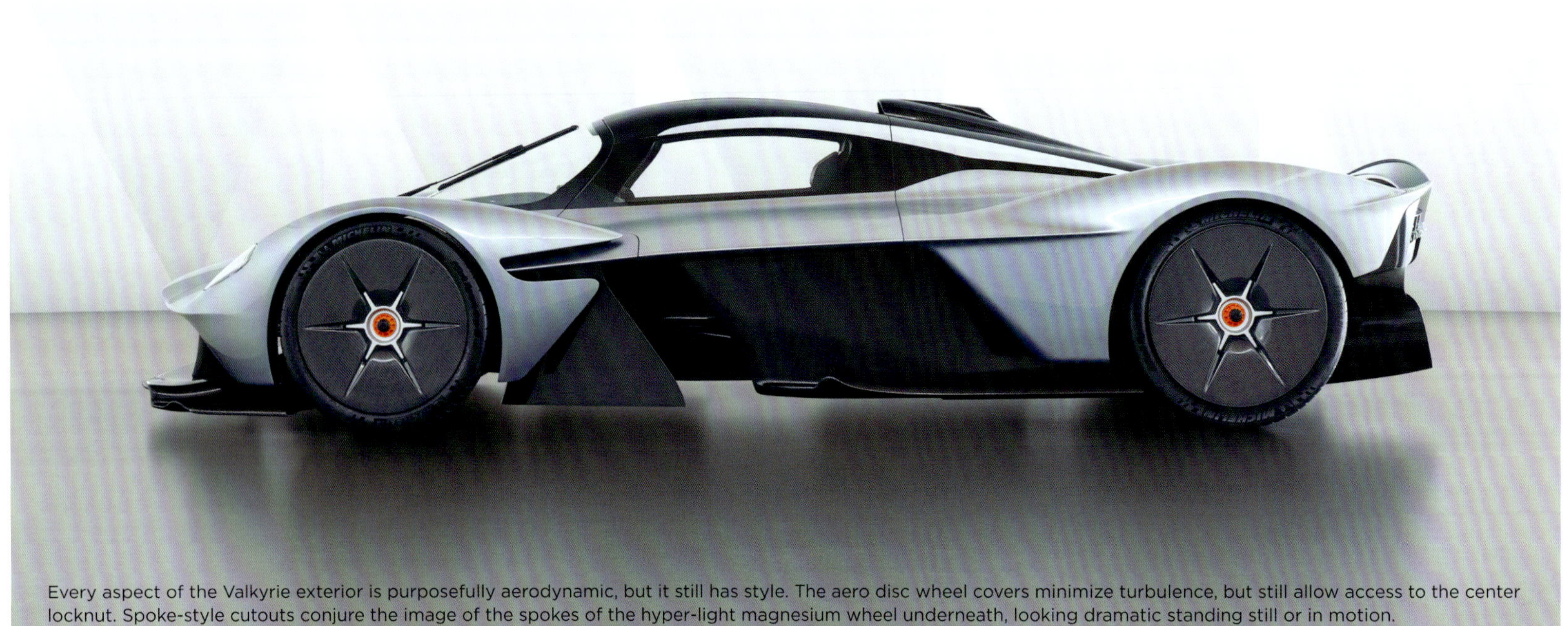

Every aspect of the Valkyrie exterior is purposefully aerodynamic, but it still has style. The aero disc wheel covers minimize turbulence, but still allow access to the center locknut. Spoke-style cutouts conjure the image of the spokes of the hyper-light magnesium wheel underneath, looking dramatic standing still or in motion.

There's stark, and then there's the Valkyrie's minimalist interior appointments. Concessions to comfort mostly consist of the "keep sharp edges from cutting people" standard, as it should be. Clean, purposeful, and uncompromised, the Valkyrie's intentions are clear.

ASTON MARTIN AUTOMOTIVE

Aston Martin has had its share of lean times. The cars themselves were rarely in doubt, but since its inception in 1913, it has had its fair share of existential threats. Almost every decade, Aston Martin was in the hands of a new investment group, and consistent leadership (and product) was hard to come by.

But in 1987, Ford bought 75% of the company (reaching full ownership in 1993), meaning the company finally had the stability to produce great cars consistently. The best part was that as a successful brand with a racing pedigree, Ford could start getting back into racing, both with GT3 spec racers and ultimately Formula 1.

As a sporting luxury brand, when the hypercar market proved to be growing, Aston Martin smartly capitalized on its engineering and history, and began producing hypercars that have no trouble finding an audience willing to snap them up.

Aston Martin Vulcan

Acceleration: 0–60 2.9 seconds

Torque: 575 lb-ft

Power output: 820bhp

Production years: 2015–2016

Production numbers: 24

Engine: 7.0 liter V12, naturally aspirated

Weight: 2,976 lbs dry

Price: USD $2,300,000

Aston Martin's first hypercar was the Vulcan. The company had produced a fantastic street car called the One-77 in 2012, a carbon-chassis special with an exterior design that closely resembled the gorgeous street-legal Vantage and Vanquish from that era. With only 77 made, that model convinced Aston that there was a viable market for exotic, limited-production cars to explore.

First produced in 2015, the Vulcan abides by a minimalist aesthetic for its specification, as befits what is essentially a race car. It was built by Aston as a track-only vehicle. It has an aluminum chassis with carbon fiber body panels and uses a 7.0 liter V12 engine based on the racing engine used in Aston Martin's Vantage GT3 cars. Inside, the sparse interior is light on equipment but sports a rotary controller to select the level of power (three stages resulting in 500hp, 675hp, or the maximum 832hp). With DSSV's multimatic spool valve dampers and carbon ceramic brakes, the hardware goes along with a sculpted body designed to produce enough downforce to work on the track. The aero package includes dive planes, an underbody diffuser, and a massive rear wing, all of which look as dramatic as they are effective.

The Vulcan was never road legal, like many of the exclusive hypercars from this era. But Aston Martin never imposed limitations about where the Vulcan could be garaged, unlike comparable Ferrari track-only specials that were kept by the company.

When set to full power via the driver adjustable rotary knob, the Vulcan hits 0–60 in under three seconds. The Vulcan has benefitted from its relatively simple but powerful naturally aspirated engine, dispelling the need for turbos or electric assistance.

ASTON MARTIN AUTOMOTIVE

The Vulcan was designed by Aston Martin Creative Officer Marek Reichman and was inspired by the Aston Martin Vantage, DB9, and One-77 models. After the Vulcan, Aston Martin went on to green-light a hypercar conceived and designed by their Formula 1 team's chief officers. The company continued to find buyers that valued its racing pedigree as well as its overall technical proficiency. While its first project turned out to be successful, there was never any guarantee of continued commercial success. In hindsight, it's easy to see how unnecessary any lingering concerns might have been, and the company's success ultimately informed the decision to offer a couple of options in the segment with the next projects.

Bugatti Bolide

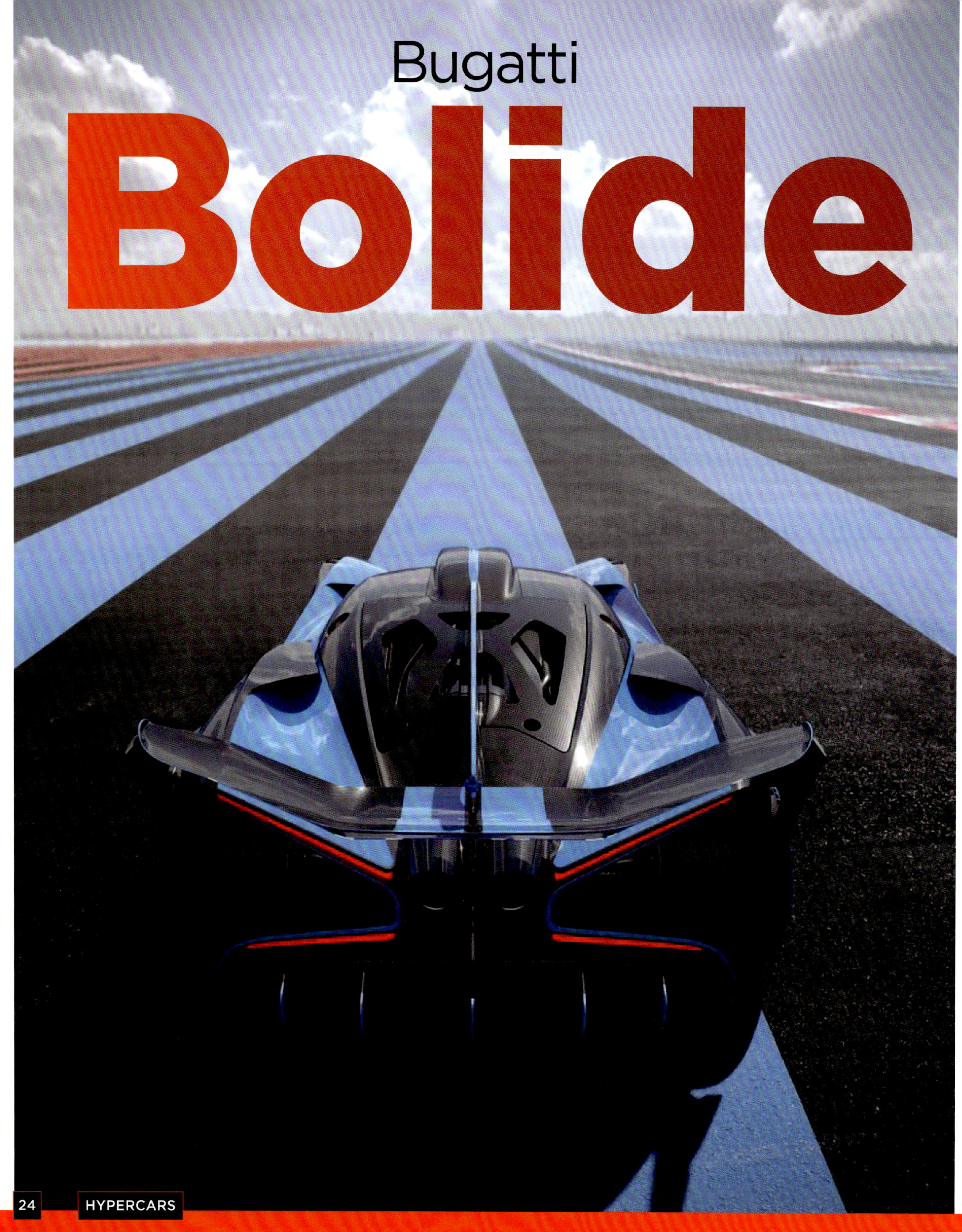

The Bolide is Bugatti's entry into the track-only hypercar segment, where concessions to street-going comfort are swept aside. In the 21st century, Bugatti has been the standard by which other manufacturers' street-going GT hypercars have been judged. Bugatti's competition history made a track hypercar like the Bolide a logical entry into the market.

The incredible W16 quad-turbocharged engine, the heart of the modern Bugatti, deserves this kind of showcase. With the lack of heavy luxury accoutrements found in the GT cars, the Bolide was going to be rapid, but Bugatti didn't just strip out a Chiron and leave it at that. It started with a titanium chassis built in collaboration with race specialists Dallara. The X-shaped monocoque was inspired by the Bell X-1 aircraft and built to FIA Le Mans series specifications. Along with carbon fiber body panels to keep weight to a minimum, the Bolide's exterior ensures competition-level downforce at speed, and the result is a suitably dramatic exterior.

The end result is staggering. The production version of the Bolide was rated at 1,578hp with a torque figure of 1,180 lb-ft at 2,250 rpm. Suitably impressive figures, but the final critical ingredient is actually the subtraction—a curb weight of 2,733 pounds. In context, a Chiron sporting the same dimensions and drivetrain weighs 4,400 pounds. With so much less weight to handle, the performance numbers back up the promise of the looks. 0 to 100 km/h takes 2.2 seconds, to 200 km/h takes 5.4 seconds, and to 300 km/h takes only 11.5 seconds.

Bugatti limited Bolide production to 40 units, but didn't waste time delivering them to the customers at the beginning of 2024, less than a year after first revealing the production version to the public.

Acceleration: 0–62mph 2.7 seconds

Torque: 1,180 lb-ft

Power output: 1,578hp

Production years: 2024

Production numbers: 40

Engine: 8.0 liter, quad-turbocharged W16

Weight: 2,733 lbs

Price: approx. USD $4,400,000

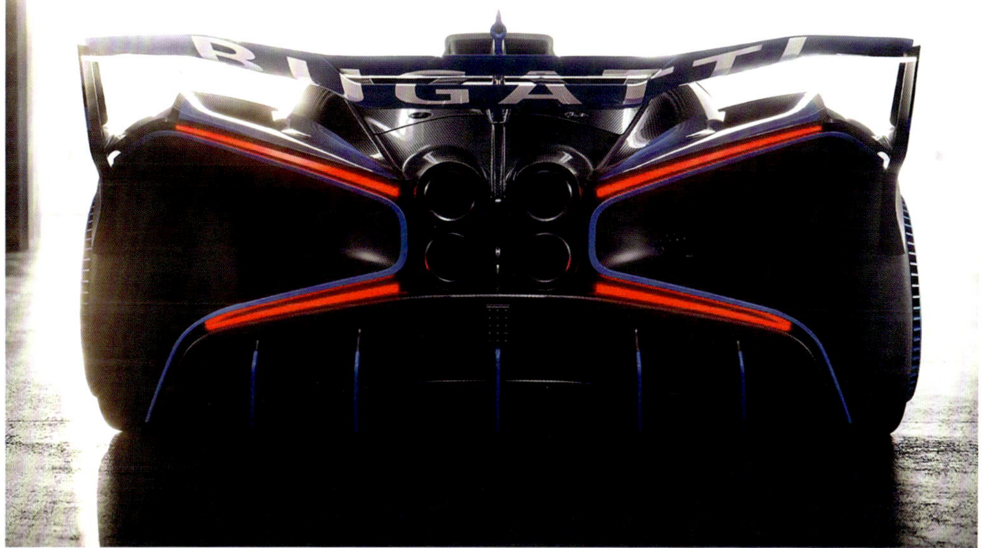

Thanks to its lightweight chassis and increased power, the Bolide manages to put serious distance on a Chiron in acceleration. 0–124mph at 5.4 seconds shaves a second off the Chiron, while 0–186mph occurs in 11.5 seconds.

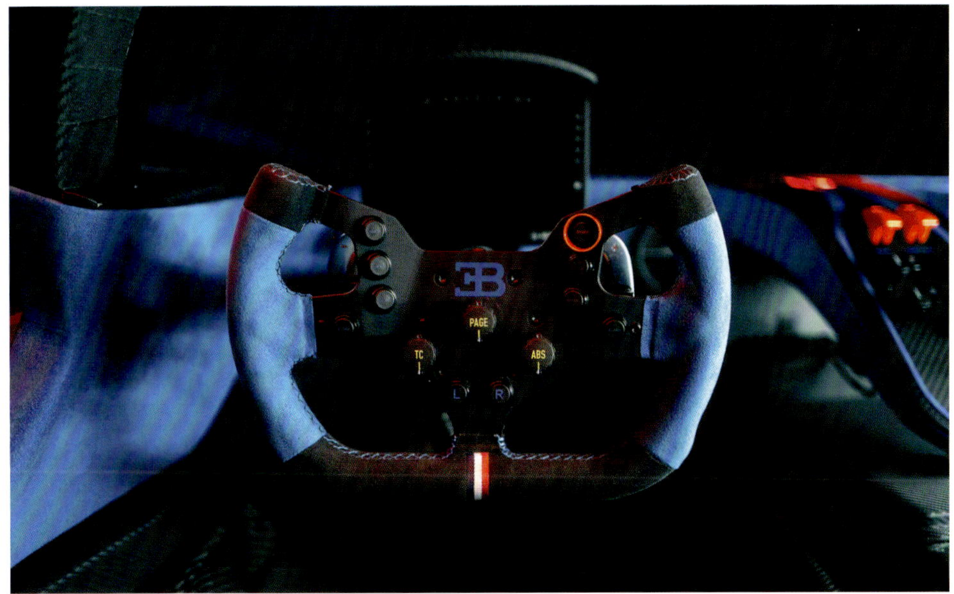

BUGATTI AUTOMOTIVE

One of the most important legends in the history of the automobile, Bugatti has seen its fortunes rise and fall. One of the earliest participants in racing, the marque not only consistently made winning race cars, but also produced luxury machines in the 1920s and 1930s that continue to be some of the most valuable in the world. But those achievements didn't protect the company during harder times. Attempts to revive it proved difficult.

It could be argued that the modern iteration of Bugatti has set the standard for the hypercar, starting with the Veyron. This model produced class-leading statistics and raised the bar for durability and consistency, much of this thanks to the engineering (and financial) might of the parent company, Volkswagen Audi Group. And for VWAG CEO Ferdinand Pïech, the Bugatti brand was a critical piece in establishing the company as the best in the world in every category, under multiple brands, with Bugatti representing the cost-no-object upper echelon.

Bugatti Chiron

The Chiron's quad-turbocharged 8.0 liter W16 engine developed an astonishing 1,500 horsepower and 1,180 pound-feet of torque—enough for a 0–60mph time of 2.4 seconds and an electronically limited top speed of 261mph. A Haldex all-wheel drive system got all that power to the road with the least amount of drama. The Chiron set a world record by accelerating 0 to 400km/h (248mph) and then braking to a stop in 41.96 seconds. That record was quickly bettered by Koenigsegg, but it was still a remarkable accomplishment. The base price for the Chiron was just over $3,000,000 in 2022. As expected at that price, there was no visible plastic in the cockpit—only top-grade leather and metal. The Chiron was more refined and quieter than its predecessor, the Bugatti Veyron, and was also surprisingly docile at low speeds.

BUGATTI AUTOMOTIVE

As the successor to the Veyron, the Chiron had high expectations to meet coming into the market. Replacing the standard-bearer in the hypercar market meant there had to be a clear improvement across the board, in every aspect, or it would be viewed as a failure. But the Chiron managed that expectation, through refinement of the Veyron's original mandate, producing this leaner-looking hypercar that built on the Veyron's success.

Even with its incredible improvements, the Chiron is proof that the world has become used to staggering performances. That's mostly the Veyron's fault. Despite being rated at just under 1,500hp, these numbers are now expected in the hypercar category—almost taken for granted, at this point. That stands in stark relief to the Veyron's 1,000+ hp figure, which contemporary observers initially found hard to believe. We have Ferdinand Pïech to thank for setting goals that once seemed impossible.

Acceleration: 0–124mph in 6.5 seconds, and 0–186mph in 13.6 seconds

Torque: 1,600 lb-ft base

Power output: 1,479hp base

Production years: 2016–2024

Production numbers: 500

Engine: 8.0 liter quad-turbocharged W16

Weight: 4,400 lbs base

Price: from USD $2,900,000 up

Bugatti Divo

Bugatti's Divo is a driver-oriented hypercar that is based on the Chiron platform, but modified enough to justify a different name. For this model, Bugatti chose to name it after Albert Divo, the French racing driver who piloted Bugattis to victory in the Targa Florio in 1928 and 1929. The design was inspired by their Type 57, from the 1930s.

Bugatti took the Chiron platform, deemphasized the GT aspects and focused on the sport. With a dorsal fin that gave it a Le Mans prototype silhouette, a full rear wing, winglets, and NACA ducts, the Divo maximized airflow management for high-speed downforce and stability, resulting in a form that is more dramatic than the elegant but relatively restrained Chiron.

The running gear for the Divo is suitably reengineered for a tauter, more athletic demeanor. Stiffer shocks and higher spring rates accompany a more aggressive negative camber specification for the suspension, and the more aggressive bodywork creates more downforce than that of the Chiron. Top speed is limited (if one can say that with a straight face) to 236mph, as the suspension modification puts more strain on the tires, creating more heat. But the upgrades make a difference, as the Divo manages significantly better lap times on track compared to the Chiron.

The interior of the Divo is essentially a Chiron with more sporting details: more aggressive seats featuring grippy Alcantara inserts, carbon fiber trim instead of shiny metals, and all the normal subtle changes for the mission—but an incredible amount of subtle.

Acceleration: 0–60mph 2.3 seconds
Torque: 1,180 lb-ft
Power output: 1,500hp
Production years: 2019–2021
Production numbers: 40
Engine: 8.0 liter quad-turbocharged W16
Weight: est. 4,323 lbs
Price: USD $5,800,000

With a top speed limited to 236mph, the Divo's focus on track-tuned suspension and more downforce meant that acceleration numbers were down across the board. But by Bugatti's own reckoning, the Divo was a massive eight seconds faster around the Nardo test track than the Chiron.

The Divo's aerodynamic work resulted in 1,005 pounds of downforce at speed, almost 200 pounds more than the Chiron. Every aspect of the exterior bodywork is more upright and aggressive, with streamlining for top speed no longer the priority.

BUGATTI AUTOMOTIVE

If the VW Audi Group is good at anything, it is the subtle industrial art of platform sharing. It's an economical approach: One basic, malleable chassis can be the basis for multiple models across different brands. Yet, engineered well and with proper differences in materials and drivetrains, the results feel distinctly different from each other, avoiding the stigma of "badge engineering."

But the Bugatti Chiron platform is one of the rare exceptions for the company, as it shares the platform with nothing else. Not an Audi, not a Porsche—it stands alone.

That said, this GT platform is more than good enough to support multiple variations on the Bugatti theme. Whether it's a coupe, open roof, luxury appointments, or a driver-oriented sport specification, the company knows how to create a base that accommodates many different missions.

Bugatti Tourbillon

As the latest installment in this century for Bugatti, the lead-up to the full public reveal of this hypercar had been the subject of some scrutiny. For the better part of two decades, every model had been equipped with the stunning quad turbo W16 engine, an engineering marvel that started at 1,001hp for the Veyron, and ended up with over 1,800hp in the various versions of the Chiron, Bolide, and Mistral. Observers initially assumed that Bugatti would find a way to increased power and pace via the engine.

But somehow Bugatti managed to navigate a new path, keeping a 16-cylinder motor but removing the four turbochargers. This was no revamp of the old engine; Bugatti replaced the W16 with an all-new V16 engine, aided by three Rimac-supplied electric motors. In many ways, this was a back-to-basics move for the company. Emphasizing simplification over complication, this return to a naturally aspirated motor informed the intent of the new model, as did the new name: the Tourbillon.

For watch aficionados, the word *tourbillon* refers to a watch's internal movement, specifically, rotating the balance wheel and escapement to achieve balance and minimize positional errors. The name underlines Bugatti's intent to create a more balanced, analog, and mechanical experience, yet the specs are still hypercar level: 1,800hp, 276mph top speed, and then, almost amusingly, a solid 3 mile electric-only mode. Inside, Bugatti made an effort to avoid digital screens and controls, with the navigation screen hidden when not in use. Instead, the cabin look emphasizes leather and metal, with mechanical switchgear. And, in the most direct connection to watches, the interior features an instrument package utilizing gears and movements to control the gauges, with windows to display the movement. These new gauges are important not only because of their aesthetics, but because they acknowledge that interiors dominated by screens may soon feel dated. The Tourbillon won't feel tethered to styles of the mid 2020s.

As an all-new model, the Tourbillon shares little with its predecessors but retains their design language. The new direction informs the thought process for many hypercar manufacturers today. This segment emphasizes emotional connections and a connection to the manufacturer's past. The impressive technology enhances the driving experience instead of dominating it.

Acceleration: 0–60mph est. 2.0 seconds

Torque: V16, 660 lb-ft, combined hybrid rating N/A

Power output: 1,800hp

Production years: scheduled for 2026

Production numbers: 250 scheduled

Engine: 8.3 liter V16, three electric motors

Weight: est. 4,299 lbs

Price: USD $4,000,000

With the new V16, it looks like the Tourbillon has a legitimate shot at getting under the 2.0 second barrier to 60mph. As incredible as this performance is, it's worth noting that this is the first version of this new powertrain—and that Bugatti never leaves well enough alone.

BUGATTI AUTOMOTIVE

The Tourbillon manages the near-impossible task of surpassing the mighty Chiron with an all-new means of motivation. The quad turbo W16 used in both the Veyron and Chiron had kept Bugatti at the top of the game for a solid two decades, a remarkable feat given the segment and the players involved. But the pivot away from forced induction and turbocharging is worth mentioning, because it's been a tried-and-true method of achieving big power in the 21st century while also importantly helping with emissions and pollution. The all new V16 engine is both naturally aspirated and high revving, providing a much different character with more intensity and energy, while the electric assistance provides torque and response. Both from a technical standpoint and from an emotional one, this is a savvy change in direction for the Bugatti hypercar, with insight into what to expect for the segment in the future.

If you're driving the Tourbillon, the windows for the mechanical movement of the gauges are almost dangerously distracting. Every detail in the interior emphasizes timelessness and a sense of pride in engineering.

Bugatti Veyron

The Super Sport and the Grand Vitesse versions of the Veyron, pictured here, were the enhanced variants with 1,183hp. The Grand Vitesse is the targa open-top version, while the Super Sport was a coupe (including this Orange World Record edition, with only 5 units produced).

Bugatti experienced a turn-of-the-century renaissance beginning with the Veyron and its promised 1,001 horsepower V16. Federalized models actually delivered 987 horsepower. Production began for 2005, and was limited to 50 vehicles annually. As it was now under Volkswagen control, this Bugatti revival was free of the financial limitations that killed a 1990s rebirth effort.

BUGATTI AUTOMOTIVE

For the modern era of hypercars, this was the scenery-levelling bomb of a machine that raised the bar for everyone. And to understand how it came to exist, we need to address who ran the VW Audi Group at the time and set about buying the nameplate and creating a new Bugatti: Ferdinand Pïech.

The Bugatti Veyron represented Pïech's unwavering standards. He pushed engineers to achieve seemingly impossible objectives: build an engine producing 1,000hp when nobody else was even close, and be capable of sustained 250mph cruising. The message: get it done, no excuses, and no doubting the mission! The lasting effects of that drive and determination are still evident, as Bugatti manages to improve with each model. But it bears repeating that Pïech drove them to achieve this even while they thought it could never happen.

Acceleration: 0-60 2.5 seconds

Torque: 922 lb-ft base

Power output: 1,001hp base

Production years: 2005-2015

Production numbers: 450

Engine: 8.0 liter quad-turbocharged W16

Weight: 4,052 lbs base

Price: USD $1,200,000 base

Bugatti

W16 Mistral

For the last hypercar to offer the quad turbo W16, Bugatti decided to build a dedicated roadster edition, with a final production run of 99 examples. Its name (which in French means "dominant wind") is apt for a hypercar that comes without the option for a roof. Not content to simply offer a Chiron with the roof removed, Bugatti sent the standard-setting engine off with the Mistral, with its own exterior design for the reengineered chassis that's configured around an open cockpit.

Bugatti took the opportunity to create a distinct look for the Mistral. Up front it retains the traditional Bugatti horseshoe grill opening, but taller fenders allow the headlights to be positioned horizontally instead of in a single line extending to the center grill. Along with the more upright windshield, the Mistral is better suited for a roadster style than the Chiron, and distinguishes itself visually from its platform mate successfully.

For the top, Bugatti opted not to have one at all. A more upright windshield helps with airflow. Other design elements push air around and away from the cabin. A clear rear wind deflector keeps both drafts and heat from the engine ducts from flowing uncomfortably back into the cabin. The sheer power from the W16 is certainly sufficient to keep the wind flowing at a high rate, but the Mistral is still a hypercar meant for sunny days.

Acceleration: 0-60mph 2.5 seconds

Torque: 1,180 lb-ft

Power output: 1,578hp

Production years: 2023

Production numbers: 99

Engine: 8.0 liter quad turbocharged W16

Weight: 4,359 lbs.

Price: USD $5,000,000

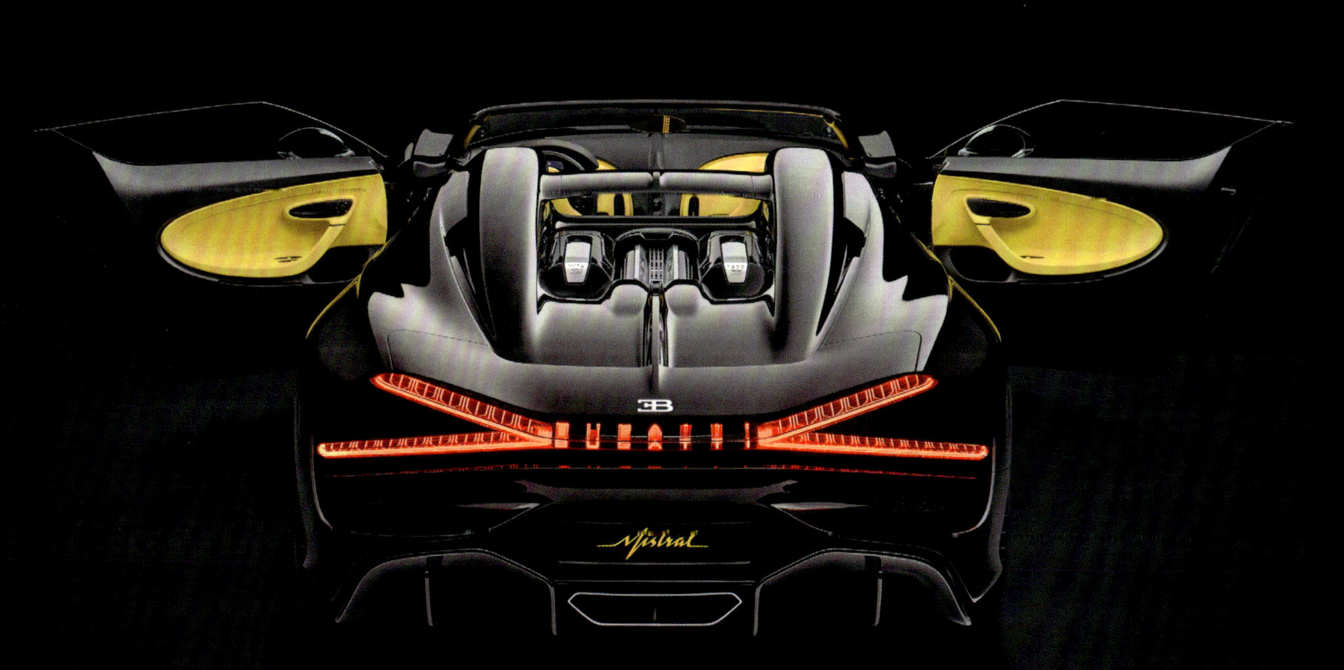

The dramatic tail lights pointing towards the center on the W16 Mistral catch your eye. They're a small detail representing the comprehensive makeover of the exterior from the base Chiron.

BUGATTI AUTOMOTIVE

For the last model using the W16 and the Chiron chassis, Bugatti did not hold back. Knowing that the replacement model would be a substantial shift away from their previous efforts, they made the Mistral a ground-up reinterpretation of their hypercar. It's worth noting here that when Ferdinand Pïech and the Volkswagen Audi Group announced the acquisition of the Bugatti name in 1998, that it was the third attempt to bring the storied company back to automotive manufacturing.

Bugatti stopped making cars in 1940. Its first attempt at a comeback was in 1951, with the lone Type 101 arriving that year. Next, in 1987, came the lovely EB110 (that lone model was produced from 1991 to 1995, resulting in 139 cars produced until the company went bankrupt). Bugatti's recent track record prompted many people to question the logic of a third try in the late 90s, but the naysayers proved to be shortsighted.

Czinger 21C

Acceleration: 0–60 1.9 seconds

Power output: combined 1,350hp

Production years: 2025

Production numbers: limited to 80

Engine: 2.9 liter twin turbocharged V8, two electric motors, one MGU

Weight: 2,960 lbs

Price: USD $2,000,000

In the hypercar segment, there is no room for a participation trophy. With competitors from some of the biggest manufacturers and the icons of motorsports, the odds of success on paper would discourage even the most capable company. This makes the Czinger 21C a standout, as the result of true engineering know-how and determination from the father-son duo that brought this car to life.

Utilizing their 3D printing experience building parts for mainstream manufacturers, the 21C's designers conceived and produced their model entirely in-house. With a fighter jet seating arrangement featuring a center driving position with the passenger directly behind, the 21C makes the proper visual statement. The chassis, body, and drivetrain are all unique to Czinger, and the specifications are impressive, starting with the means of propulsion. The combustion engine is a 2.9 liter V8, twin turbocharged, rear-mounted, and running through a seven-speed dual clutch automatic transmission to the rear wheels. Two hub-mounted electric motors are mounted to the front wheels, along with an axial flux Motor Generator Unit to produce electricity. The hybrid system produces a combined 1,350hp, with the ICE motor providing 950hp at 11,500 rpm, and the two electric hub motors splitting the extra 400hp between them.

There are currently three variants of the 21C to choose from. The 21C V Max, pictured above, features a longer tail and less downforce aero, along with aero wheel discs, to achieve a higher top speed.

CZINGER AUTOMOTIVE

For a company specializing in industrial design and manufacturing, the path to automotive design was an organic one. The Czinger 21C is a showcase for the father-and-son team's ability to create 3D printed design parts and pieces with a typical engineer's eye for detail, but with the passion and energy that comes from creating a job for oneself instead of applying for one.

The family's engineering firm, Divergent, already produces chassis and related assemblies for other major manufacturers, and they are disruptors in the best sense of the word. Their 3D modeling and printing processes streamline the manufacturing process, using computer design technology to change how modern cars are constructed. The 21C is a showcase for what this process is capable of, and how it can show established automakers to approach their business with a fresh, outsiders' perspective.

De Tomaso P72

The P72 is the first De Tomaso model available in decades, yet its creation follows De Tomaso history perfectly. Based on an existing chassis built by Apollo, the P72 pays homage to a 1960s project collaboration with Carroll Shelby. In an attempt to improve the speed of the De Tomaso Vallelunga, Shelby was brought on board to fix the issue, which to Shelby meant: grab a Ford V8 engine and problem solved. Along with help from Peter Brock and Medardo Fantuzzi on the exterior design, the finished prototype was called the P70. Unfortunately, Shelby was wooed away by Ford to help them on their Ford GT Le Mans project—which for Shelby was clearly a good move, in retrospect—and the lovely P70 never saw completion in that form.

Consider this the make-up test. The De Tomaso P72 uses a carbon fiber monocoque as the basis for an analog, immersive hypercar. It is powered by a Ford engine, of course (this time a 5.0 liter supercharged V8 with 750hp). De Tomaso chose to use a six-speed manual transmission (the old-school description for manual, which involves three pedals with no automated shifting) and analog gauges with an interior devoid of screens for a fully classic experience. Interior detailing also includes rose-gold metal accents and gauge surrounds matched with diamond stitched leather, fully covering the carbon chassis with a vintage look.

The exterior, with raised haunches and tight bodywork around the canopy, has done a masterful job evoking the shape of a real 1960s Le Mans prototype, looking nothing like a modern hypercar and making effective use of LED taillights in round assemblies to imitate old-school incandescent taillights from another era.

Torque: 664 lb-ft

Power output: 750hp

Production years: 2025

Production numbers: limited to 72

Engine: 5.0 liter supercharged V8

Price: USD $1,450,000

The P72 isn't quite as aerodynamically efficient as many of its competitors—it doesn't employ the newer methods for increasing downforce. Instead, there is a still-slippery but more evocative shape derived from '60s icons, equipped with spoilers front and rear to keep it grounded at speed.

DE TOMASO AUTOMOTIVE

Alejandro De Tomaso originally founded the company bearing his name in 1959. He started with racing prototypes and managed to establish name recognition despite an inconsistent production history. The company has produced notable cars under its own name while also handling manufacturing for other companies. De Tomaso even took over Maserati from the mid 1970s to the mid 1990s, a perfect example of an old-school small company thriving while building memorable cars for long stretches.

Staying in business over the years has proven difficult—a common issue for small-batch sports cars not absorbed by or affiliated with larger manufacturers. Moving in and out of solvency can almost seem like a ritual. But for the last decade, the hypercar market has garnered enough sales to warrant investment, and this is how the De Tomaso name has managed to step into the light yet again.

Ferrari

812 Competizione

The 812 Competizione signifies the end of one of the most glorious eras in automotive history: the reign of the 12-cylinder Ferrari GT. For enthusiasts of every age group, Ferrari's evocative GTs have long been the enduring north star for achievement, consistently not only among the strongest performers, but also the most desirable, even as challengers have come and gone. No matter what the competition tried, Ferrari had a response, using V12 or flat 12-cylinder engines along with front or mid engine layouts, and always draped in the best bodywork.

With the Competizione, Ferrari produced its last non-hybrid, naturally aspirated V12, and sent it off properly. Based on the already superlative 812 Superfast, Ferrari produced a 6.5 liter naturally aspirated V12, in this iteration producing 819hp, with a redline of 9,500 rpm (a "limit" so elevated that it caused a visceral reaction just from the idea of experiencing it in person).

The Competizione itself is a special version of the already special 812 Superfast. So while the improvement is in some ways incremental from a great "basic" model, visual flair through ground effects and details bolster its specialness. The notable difference for the Competizione might be the rear window—as in the complete lack of one. For even more carefully managed airflow, the back light has a cover with curved foils to assist with downforce at speed, with a small fin equipped with a rear-facing camera in place of the glass.

Since the standard 812 Superfast exists as a GT, the Competizione tilts in favor of pace over comfort, with minimal concession to driver isolation from the road. But even considering the fact that it is a powerful rear-wheel drive hypercar, the platform makes it easier to run than would be expected. Between its evenly distributed weight balance, and the smooth, consistent power produced by the naturally aspirated V12 throughout the rev range, the 812 Competizione manages to qualify as an "easy" hypercar.

Acceleration: 0–60mph 2.6 seconds

Torque: 510 lb-ft

Power output: 819hp

Production years: 2022

Production numbers: 1,598 (999 coupes, 599 Apertas)

Engine: 6.5 liter V12

Weight: 3,700 lbs

Price: USD $602,000

While the Competizione is impressive, there's always room for an open-air version. The yellow example shown here is the Competizione A, the targa top version that complements the coupe version nicely.

FERRARI AUTOMOTIVE

As the hypercar segment continues to grow, standing out in the crowd becomes increasingly difficult, especially as performance numbers, dramatic styling, and incredible detail inspires manufacturers to greater and greater heights. But even with that being the case, everybody knows there is one true king of the hill, and of course it's Ferrari. Manufacturers might have any combination of the necessary ingredients to compete—performance, looks, history, a racing pedigree—but by any metric, no other company manages to hit that *summa cum laude* level of excellence in every category as Enzo Ferrari's legendary company does repeatedly. While it had its share of financial crises, and not every model it manufactured was a success, Ferrari has managed to produce cars (both for the street and for competition), that stand out not just as amazing machines, but as cultural icons. Even more impressively, the company has managed to stay true to the mission first laid out by its founder, while escaping the kind of platform sharing with sister companies that could dilute the brand.

Ferrari Daytona SP3

When you're Ferrari, chassis sharing is more than just an economical decision. In the case of its hypercars, it's an elite game of mix and match, creating new models for maximum effect, which you then casually drape with an evocative design to create a stunning product. The SP3 utilized the chassis from the Aperta, blessed it with a V12 running 812 Competizione specification, then wrapped it in a roadster design that recalls the legendary 330 P4 race cars from the late 1960s. With a removable carbon fiber roof and a minimalist interior layout, the SP3 is an analog old-school hypercar, with no turbos or electric motors, relying on its most powerful V12 and reduced weight for the purest version of a Ferrari experience.

This palate-cleansing simplicity, by an historically important company like Ferrari, makes a great alternative to its incredible but technologically complex LaFerrari. Instead of utilizing all of the knowledge gained from the F1 program, as advanced and forward-thinking as it is, the SP3 is for the owner looking for the core elements that made Ferraris great for decades. At a price exceeding USD $2,200,000, and limited to 599 cars, the SP3 was meant for the long-time Ferrari customer. This model was unavailable to the mass market and could be purchased invitation-only.

On its own, it's a special machine. But it speaks to Ferrari's success that it can offer such distinctly different cars in the hypercar segment at the same time and give its best clients such specific choices.

Acceleration: 0–60mph 2.6 seconds

Torque: 510 lb-ft

Power output: 819hp

Production numbers: 599

Engine: 6.5 liter NA V12

Weight: 3,450 lbs

Price: USD $2,224,000

FERRARI AUTOMOTIVE

If your directive as a Ferrari designer is to bring some visual lineage to your new hypercar, Ferrari has a back catalog that makes the job an easy one. In this case, Ferrari looked to a mix from their 60s era, specifically the 330 P4 from 1967 and the 250 P5 Pininfarina concept car for the vertical slats in the front and rear.

The SP3 comes along right when Ferrari's design direction has started to move away from its recent hard-edged emphasis, and back towards more flowing lines and body elements reminiscent of their 1960s and 1970s era, with both Pininfarina and Bertone design house elements making their way back into favor.

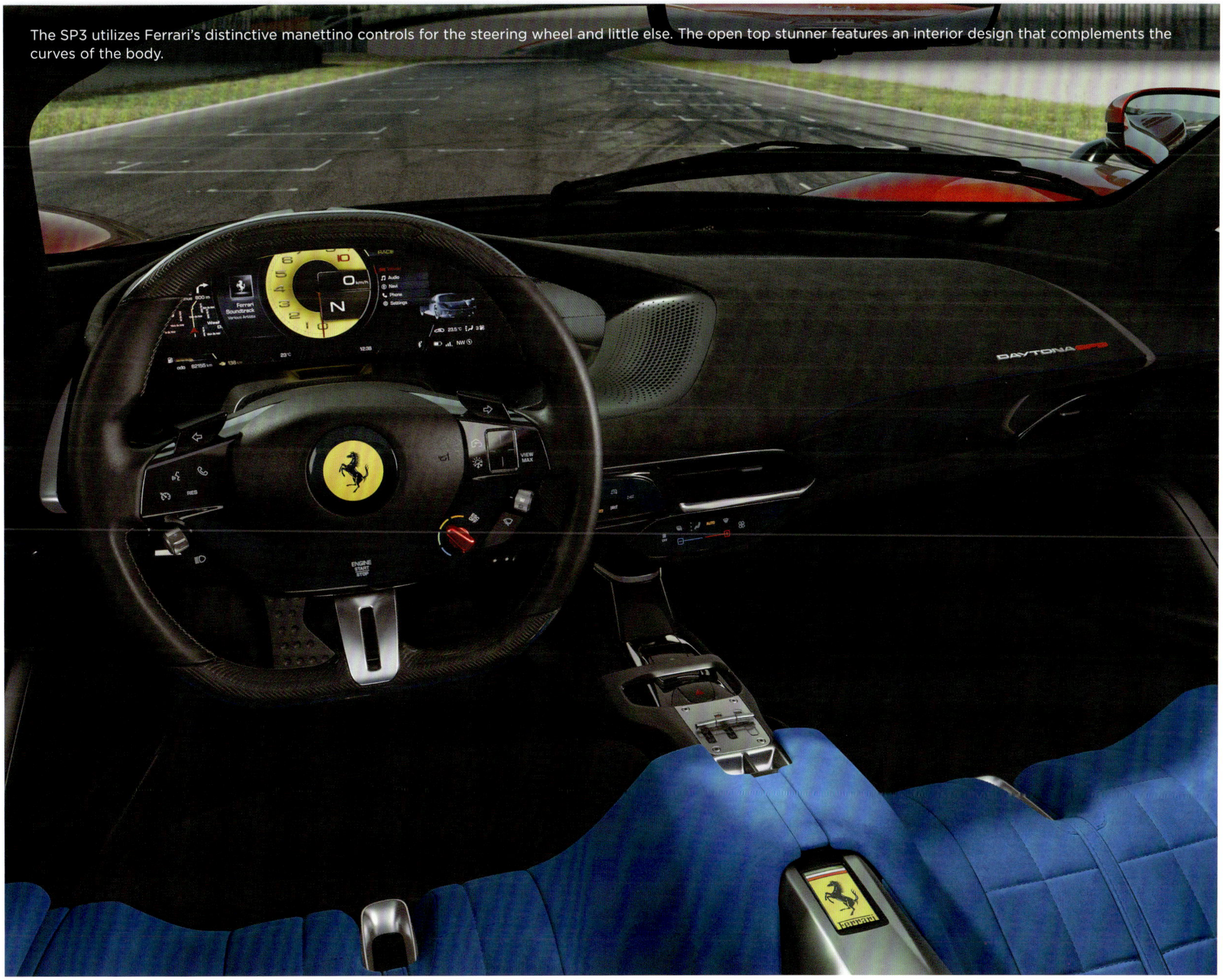

The SP3 utilizes Ferrari's distinctive manettino controls for the steering wheel and little else. The open top stunner features an interior design that complements the curves of the body.

Ferrari F80

As the latest entry in the hybrid hypercar segment, the F80 builds on the strengths of the LaFerrari original, with scarcely credible power numbers: it is the most powerful roadgoing Ferrari ever made. Drawing directly from its Formula 1 developmental experience, Ferrari continues to improve on packaging efficiency by reducing the size of the combustion engine with each generation, while simultaneously increasing horsepower and acceleration figures. This time around, it's a twin turbo V6 that produces 888hp, mated to electric motors, resulting in 1,184 combined hp.

The exterior of the F80 is assuredly functional in nature, providing the necessary ducting to keep the motors cool, the eye-opening 2,300-plus pounds of aero downforce at 155mph for staying in contact with the road, and a full complement of electronically adjustable wings and airflow both over and under the car. But from a design standpoint, while the F80 is futuristic in overall concept, it breaks away from a lot of the recent Ferrari designs where razor sharp straight edges dominate.

The rising curves over the top of the wheel openings give the exterior a less clinical look while they emphasize the wheel itself, adding to the visual drama. Visual drama also seems the goal of the blackout panel that sits between the headlight apertures, recalling the look of the 365 GTB Daytona. In sum, the F80 presents a strong design tie-in to its forebears without merely copying them.

Acceleration: 0–60mph 2.1 seconds

Torque: 793 lb-ft

Power output: 1,186hp

Production years: beginning late 2025

Weight: est. 3,500 lbs

Price: est. USD $4,000,000

The lineage that ties the F80 to predecessors like the F50 is clear when viewed from above, but in terms of ability the F80 dominates. The compact V6 produces more power on its own than the F50's V12, and when paired with its electric motors, practically doubles that.

FERRARI AUTOMOTIVE

Design for Ferrari's lineup is currently under the direction of Flavio Manzoni, who has held the position since 2010. Given Ferrari's history and collaborations with Italy's legendary design houses, Manzoni has much to live up to. In the hypercar segment, managing airflow is obviously a priority to ensure both stability and thermal efficiency—Manzoni's responsibility for making Ferrari's models instantly recognizable and also meeting hypercar standards is a daunting task.

While much of the 2010s saw an emphasis on designing models with hard edges, the latest models have seen a return to the softer shapes on critical sections of the design. This extends to the F80, which merges those edges and curves just enough to suggest Ferrari lineage without being simply a retro attempt.

What's easy to forget is that Ferrari isn't light on variety. There are over ten models available at this point, and they all manage to have their own identity while still carrying enough visual cues to signify the brand visually.

The interior features a red driver's seat and a black passenger's seat, making the priority obvious. The instrument and control panels do away with screens dominating the view, resulting in a much less technological feel, and again echoing past designs.

Ferrari

LaFerrari

Ferrari would probably be the last make expected to sell a hybrid, but the LaFerrari was no ordinary hybrid—it combined a 788hp V12 with a 161hp electric motor for a total 950hp. Introduced for 2013, the LaFerrari hybrid was even faster than Ferrari's celebrated 2003–04 Enzo model—it could rocket from 0–60mph in less than three seconds and hit a top speed of 217mph. Plus, the weight of the low-mounted battery packs lowered the car's center of gravity and improved handling. The LaFerrari's price tag was a cool $1.4 million, but Ferrari had no trouble selling 500 coupes, as well as 210 Aperta convertible versions. The final LaFerrari Aperta was sold at an auction in 2017 for $9.96 million, with proceeds supporting the Save the Children charity.

Acceleration: 0–60mph 2.5 seconds

Torque: 715 lb-ft (combined)

Power output: 950hp (combined)

Production years: 2013–2018

Production numbers: 499 coupes, 210 Apertas

Engine: 6.3 liter V12, 1 AC electric motor

Weight: 3,489 lbs

Price: USD $1,420,000

The lean bodywork remains both purposeful and instantly recognizable as a Ferrari. Dual rear tail lights with recessed cutouts frame a rear spoiler that gracefully curves up at the center, with neatly integrated diffuser and exhaust outlets along the bottom.

FERRARI AUTOMOTIVE

The LaFerrari was a tipping point for the manufacturer, as it began to adapt to an electric hybrid future with an emphasis on power over economy. Thanks to its previous work in Formula 1, this was a logical step forward for Ferrari. It applied lessons learned in synchronizing the V12 with a powerful electric motor to power its latest hyper car. The electric motor proved a great complement to the V12, of course, by providing "torque fill" (utilizing the electric motor's ability to provide instant torque when the V12 was at low revs) resulting in much quicker acceleration across the board. Torque fill has become a handy catchphrase, perfectly describing the sensation from the extra grunt coming out of slow speed turns with this drivetrain.

Ferrari
SF90 XX Stradale

At its introduction, Ferrari's SF90 established itself as one of the fastest V8 Ferraris of all time. Blisteringly quick and smooth with its mild hybrid setup, it was a logical progression from the LaFerrari, utilizing electric motors while stepping down from the V12 to a twin turbo V8. Its performance exceeded the public's expectations.

Of course, the time soon came for a quicker version variant. The SF90 XX Stradale is exactly that: a showcase for Ferrari's advancement in the hybrid segment, with more than 1,000hp for the street. What's interesting is the car's name. XX has, for Ferrari, usually meant a special track-only edition of an existing road car (one that owners wouldn't even keep for themselves). Maintained by Ferrari, the XX program was available only to the most loyal of customers, and the cars themselves were only brought out for special events at racetracks, under the watchful eye of Ferrari the whole time.

This time, the car is road legal. It is a substantially improved version of the "standard" SF90. Power rises only slightly—though in going from 986hp combined to 1,016hp, breaking into the four-digit power range is still eye-opening. Along with the power increase, a larger fixed rear wing and additional sculpting of the existing active aero result in downforce that is doubled compared to the standard model. The interior features fixed-back racing bucket seats and a noticeable lack of carpeting. The exposed carbon and bare floors emphasize the track-oriented mission of the XX Stradale. While it won't be seen running amateur events frequently, it does take a solid step forward in ability compared to its already enormously capable GT-oriented sibling.

Acceleration: 0–60mph 1.9 seconds

Torque: 590 lb-ft

Power output: 1,016hp

Production years: 2025

Engine: 4.0 liter twin turbo V8; 3 permanent magnet AC electric motors (two front, one rear)

Weight: 3,800 lbs

Price: USD $890,000

The subtle sculpting of the back deck of the standard SF90 is set aside for more grip, starting with the large fixed wing. An extended tail section and diffuser, plus a movable lower wing and Gurney lip for adjustment at speed, aid in keeping the back wheels planted.

FERRARI AUTOMOTIVE

While the Stradale SF90 is street legal, the previous XX variants for Ferrari provided their owners with an immersive experience in Ferrari racing that other manufacturers subsequently began to imitate. One of the best examples of this was the Ferrari FXX, the race-prepped variant of the Enzo. Produced during the height of Ferrari's dominance in Formula 1 (and thanks in part to racing legend Michael Schumacher), the FXX was an invitation-only offering.

A few lucky customers got to participate in track events, driving FXXs maintained by Ferrari. The cars were equipped with on-board telemetry so that the laps recorded could be used by Ferrari to aid in performance development. Only 30 FXXs were made, along with one reserved for Michael Schumacher.

Ford GT

Acceleration: 0–60mph 2.9 seconds

Torque: 550 lb-ft

Power output: 647hp

Production years: 2016–2022

Production numbers: 1,350

Engine: 3.0 liter, twin turbo V6

Weight: 3,055 pounds

Price: USD $500,000

To celebrate the 50th anniversary of the Ford GT40's historic 1966 Le Mans victory, Ford designed an all-new GT racecar for the 2016 24 Hours of Le Mans. The new GTs did their legendary forebears proud, finishing first, third, fourth, and ninth in the GTE Pro Class. The production GT was closely related to the racing version, and lacked the luxury features often found on other high-end supercars. The GT's cockpit was a tight fit for two passengers, and cargo room was almost nonexistent. The payoff was reduced weight, with race car-like performance and handling. The EcoBoost 3.5 liter V6 shared its basic engine block with the Ford F-150, but developed 647 horsepower and was capable of traveling from 0–60mph in 2.9 seconds and reaching a top speed of 216mph, according to *Car and Driver.*

Elegant yet purposeful, the Ford GT's exterior is a logical extension of the original '60s Le Mans racer. The styling cues—even without the Gulf livery—evoke the original GT Le Mans racer. But details like the incredible flying buttresses, with large channels for directing airflow, make for efficient aero management.

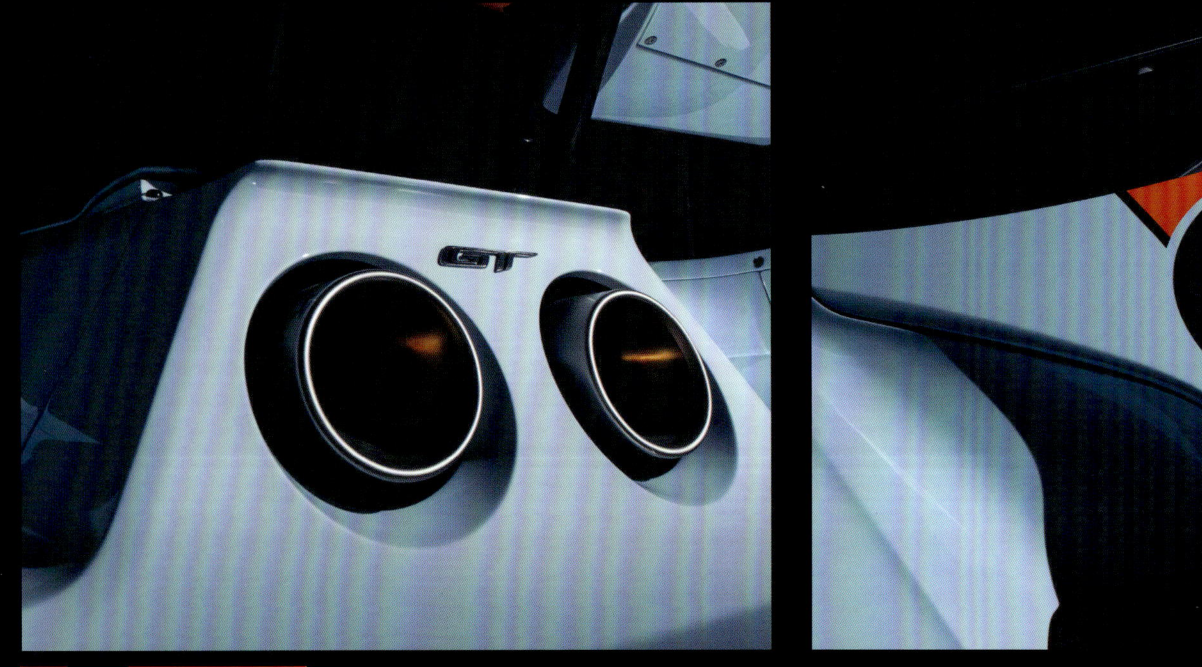

FORD AUTOMOTIVE

Ford's place in the hypercar category began with the original Ford GT and with its racing pedigree. That the original GT and the procurement of Carroll Shelby's talents in the 1960s to build a Ferrari beater was the result of Henry Ford II's widely-known grudge against Enzo Ferrari (for declining sale of the company to Ford after a long courtship) gives the origin story an extra edge that makes it compelling.

It took the finances of Ford, the know-how and experience of Shelby, and the sheer stubborn willpower of the incredible Ken Miles to design, test, and produce a car that had the ability to take on the far more experienced Ferrari in the arena. The most impressive aspect is that, while bringing back the GT nameplate just twice (and essentially starting from scratch each time to create a new street-legal hypercar), both times the end result has been a legitimate contender against the best the world has to offer.

Gordon Murray Automotive
T.33

For Gordon Murray, the legendary designer responsible for some of the world's best sports cars, the GMA T.33 is his very, very precise expression of what a hypercar should be. The two cars from his company celebrate the analog driving experience in an individualistic way.

Design-wise, the look is taut and stretched across the chassis as tightly as possible. In fact, some observers consider it delicate looking. With a wasp waist in the middle, this car is all about beautiful simplicity.

The design goes against the current grain. It focuses on the most connected possible experience for the driver, eschewing filters, turbos, superchargers, and electric assistance. Instead, it presents the naturally aspirated V12 made by Cosworth, and built to rev—and rev and rev to the sky! The redline for this magic motor is in superbike territory: 11,100 rpm, with its maximum power of 607hp occurring just below that at 10,500. Buyers are given the choice of either a six-speed manual or a dual clutch automatic, with the semi-auto being the quicker option. Yet, buyers are choosing the manual overwhelmingly at this point, and given the analog nature of the T.33, this isn't surprising!

The exterior shape maximizes downforce and airflow, particularly from the undertray and rear diffuser. Downforce is not only strong but intentionally centered towards the middle of the car, giving the driver a balanced feel. Even by hypercar standards, this car emphasizes neutrality and ease of access to its considerable power. Its unique and sonorous mechanical noise enhances the experience.

Acceleration: 0–60mph 3.0 seconds

Torque: 344 lb-ft

Power output: 607hp

Production years: 2024–2025

Production numbers: limited to 100

Engine: 3.9 liter V12

Weight: 2,403 lbs

Price: USD $2,300,000

GORDON MURRAY AUTOMOTIVE

Gordon Murray became a legend for his Formula 1 designs and engineering abilities. That background still informs his objectives for new GMA models across the board.

The new models still mirror the objectives of their legendary predecessor, the impossibly desirable McLaren F1. Murray's first opportunity to produce a street car from a clean slate was the F1. It was a staggering achievement at its introduction, with a special BMW-designed V12 with 627hp, a manual transmission, and the now signature center driving position, with passenger seats on either side of the driver for three-person hypercar carpooling!

While these seemed impossibly pricey at introduction in 1992 (USD $800,000), transaction prices currently hover at USD $20,000,000! Some claim there has been no better driver car ever made. It could be argued that the only cars to approach that ideal, since they originate from the same man, would be the GMAs.

Gordon Murray avoids excess. The weight, size, and form of the T.33 all reflect the founder's engineering priorities and philosophies. The view from the rear is clean and tidy, wrapped as tightly around the mechanicals as possible, yet the rise above the wheels still adds visual drama.

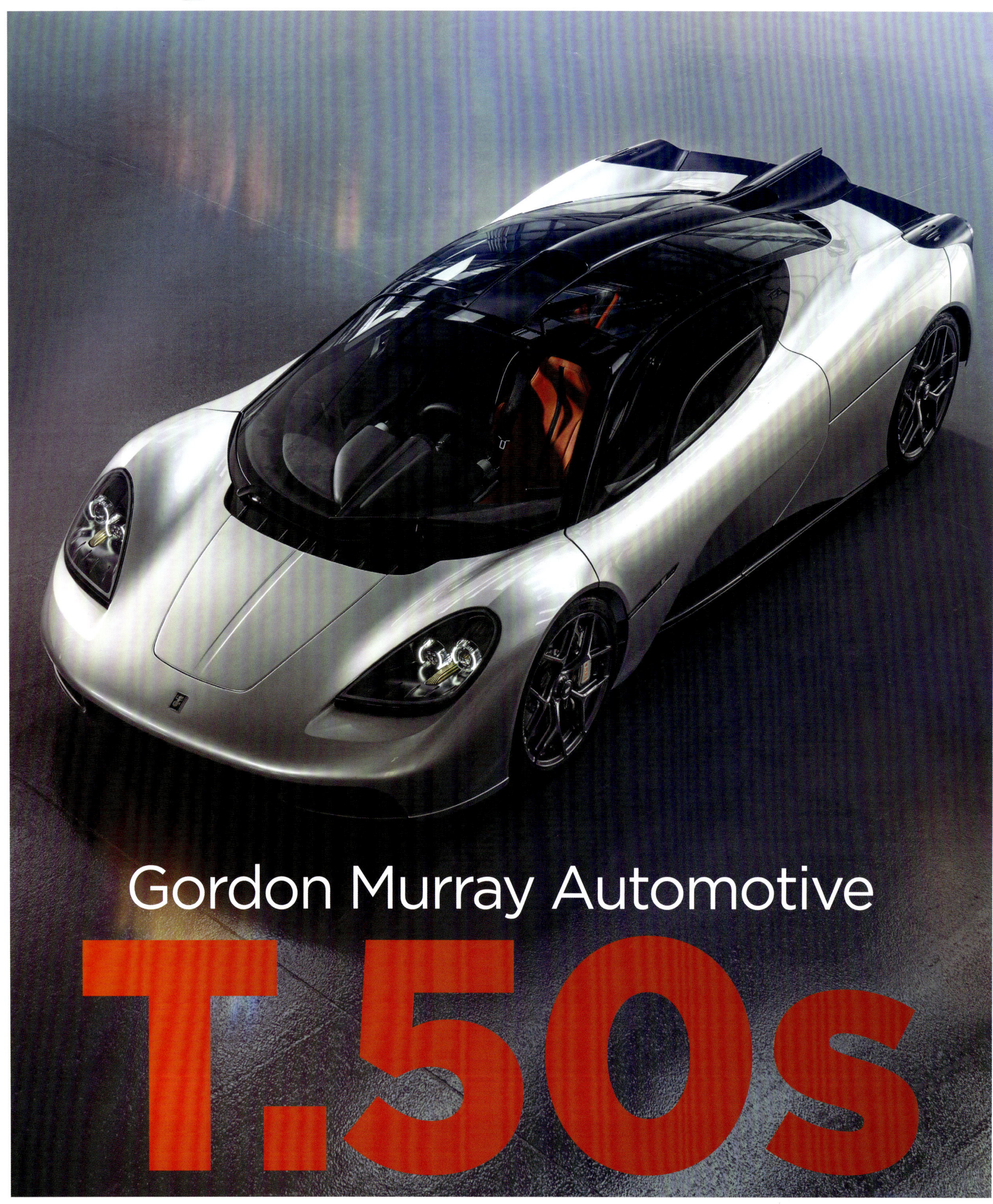

Gordon Murray Automotive T.50s

The flagship T.50s's specifications speak for themselves. It utilizes the Cosworth V12, and employs a 12,000 rpm redline. While the power is relatively modest by hypercar standards, the power to weight ratio more than compensates, along with slippery aero to go with it.

On the subject of air, the truly distinguishing feature of the T.50s has to be how it uses wind flow in a unique and active way. The rear fan is capable of spinning at as much as 7000 rpm if necessary. This allows it to pull air from underneath, creating suction no amount of flow management with diffusers could accomplish. Cockpit-adjustable for speed and location (either underneath or switched to the engine bay), the fan can help the car either achieve better grip or direct air to create an airstream beyond the end of the car to achieve better aerodynamics and a higher speed.

Inside the T.50s, the McLaren F1 DNA reveals itself clearly: a center driving position allowing two passengers to enjoy the drive. Similarly, the sole choice of a manual transmission and very little electronic intervention emphasizes the design's old school analog approach to driver enjoyment.

The uncompromising nature of the T.50s seems extreme. Yet, for suspension, Gordon Murray famously shuns the premise that a street car should be too stiff to allow driving comfort. Keeping the specification on the (relatively) plush side means some body roll in corners compared to a track day special. It also means enough suspension to absorb road irregularities and broken pavement.

In the midst of a four-digit horsepower war, the T.50s proves that there is still room for a hypercar that doesn't get in the way of driver enjoyment. Even at this level, simplicity works.

Acceleration: 0–60mph 2.7 seconds

Torque: 344 lb-ft

Production years: 2024

Production numbers: limited to 100

Engine: 3.9 liter V12

Weight: 2,176 lbs

Price: USD $3,000,000

Wasp-waisted and lean, the T.50 design elements are examples of form following function to great effect. The airflow management behind the front wheels is provided by lower cutouts in the doors, yet the result looks purposeful and dramatic, though not as dramatic as the rear-mounted fan.

GORDON MURRAY AUTOMOTIVE

Along with the smaller T.33, the T.50s reflects the philosophy of its creator, Gordon Murray. This is thanks to the fact that Murray was allowed to design without compromise. As a contrast to this success, when Murray agreed to design a supercar for Mercedes-Benz, he found himself at odds with the company on what the SLR would be. The project began with a mid-engine configuration (Murray's design preference) but the cost was deemed too expensive by Mercedes; the move to a cheaper front engine was the compromise. In order to achieve his 50/50 weight balance, Murray lengthened the nose enough for the engine to sit behind the front wheels instead of over them. This achieved the desired balance, but the lack of proportion wound up being a sticking point. It ultimately saw Murray and Daimler-Benz parting ways.

Hennessey

Venom F5

John Hennessey's company had decades of experience as an American tuner that specialized in big power. But that didn't prepare anyone for what was subsequently seen from the company. The Venom F5 is appropriately named after the highest force level for tornadoes, which not so coincidentally can exceed 300mph.

That was the target speed set for this American hypercar. It takes serious power for that to be remotely feasible. Big power isn't new for Hennessey Performance, but the heart of this hypercar is the company's own built-from-the-ground-up engine design. After many years specializing in upgrading V8s from Chevy, Ford, Cadillac, and Dodge, it designed an all-new motor. Called the Fury, it is a 6.6 liter, twin turbocharged V8, producing a stunning 1,817hp, and 1,193 lb-ft of torque. Foregoing complexity, the F5 is only rear-wheel drive, running power through a single-clutch automated manual. With a yoke style steering wheel and steering wheel-mounted shifter paddles, the F5 has the appearance of a Le Mans racer. The emphasis is on speed over luxury trim.

For the chassis, Hennessey went for a full carbon fiber monocoque and body panels, along with active aero. This has kept the weight below 3,000 pounds, while the active aero allows for the stability and downforce needed at higher speeds.

To answer any questions about its capability, Hennessey personally drove the Venom F5 to achieve a world record, recording a standing half-mile record run of 14.44 seconds at 219mph. All 24 anticipated production models have been spoken for.

Acceleration: 0–60mph 2.5 seconds

Torque: 1,193 lb-ft

Power output: 1,817hp

Production years: 2020–present

Production numbers: 24

Engine: 6.6 liter, twin turbo V8

Weight: est. 2,950 lbs

Price: USD $1,600,000

All hypercars are capable of serious speed, but Hennessy's aim for a two-way average of 300mph is still eye-popping. The namesake founder has decades of experience, so the power and capability of the F5 just might hit that target. The bodywork emphasizes high speed aero efficiency.

HENNESSEY AUTOMOTIVE

The Venom series of sports cars came from the Hennessey Special Vehicles division. The division was established in 2017 when the company decided that it was time to build vehicles from the ground up instead of modifying cars from other companies.

John Hennessey's company has a long history of getting even more power out of some of America's most powerful cars, trucks, and SUVs. What separated this company from other tuners was a willingness to work on cars from different manufacturers. So instead of sticking with just Dodge and its Viper, it would work on Chevrolet Camaros, Cadillac CTS-Vs with the GM LT supercharged V8, or build a large Ford SUV based on that company's Raptor pickup. That wide range of experience informed its move into building its own hypercars and becoming its own manufacturer of special machines.

Hennessey

Venom F5 Rev Roadster

After producing its F5 coupe from scratch, Hennessey needed to come up with another showcase for its new manufacturing division. An easy choice might have been to reengineer the structure to produce an open top version (though putting out a machine with no roof and designed to exceed 250mph might have been taking the "fresh air" concept too far).

Yet the Revolution Roadster is a great complement to the standard coupe. While that fixed roof hypercar was limited to 24 units, the Roadster has an even more exclusive forecast, with only 12 examples slated to be produced.

The Revolution adds a more track-oriented mission into the mix. It looks substantially more aggressive than the standard F5. More aggressive aero pieces for extra downforce, including dive planes and a larger, more aggressive rear wing, are paired with pronounced side skirts to add more stability to complement the aggressive suspension setup.

Employing a carbon fiber removable roof panel, the Roadster still keeps passengers out of the airstream for comfort. For sun exposure, Hennessey employs a removable carbon fiber panel with four quick-release bolts.

All told, Hennessey has managed to create five separate models from its platform, using the same engine on street- and track-oriented setups with coupe or roadster flavors.

Acceleration: 0–60mph 2.5 seconds

Torque: 1,193 lb-ft

Power output: 1,817hp

Production years: 2025

Production numbers: 12

Engine: 6.6 liter, twin turbo V8

Weight: est. 3,000 lbs

Price: USD $3,000,000

An emphasis on track performance means a drop in top speed and more concern with downforce. The expected large rear wing dominates visually. Since drag isn't a central concern, owners have the option to remove the top, adding to the sensory experience for occupants.

HENNESSEY AUTOMOTIVE

While there are many major manufacturers in the hypercar segment with budgets to allow continual testing and refinement, Hennessey has had to hustle to make its business model work. By not relying on an existing gasoline motor, or electric power, Hennessey took on the big companies all by itself. Like the major corporations, it has created variations in body style, including track and street specs, but has smartly recycled components and has just one version of their engine. With some luck and continued success, Hennessey can develop newer vehicles using its Fury engine in a wider variety of coupes, roadsters, and possibly even sedans or trucks.

Koenigsegg

Agera RS

Koenigsegg is a small, independent manufacturer based in Sweden that started building cars in the mid nineties. The Koenigsegg Agera RS turned heads with an official time of 277.9mph for a two-way average on an 11-mile stretch of highway in Nevada. Actually, the Agera RS's best time was 284.6mph, but official testing requires an average of travel in both directions. Previously, Koenigsegg broke a record set by Bugatti by accelerating 0 to 400 km/h (248mph) and then braking to a stop in 36.44 seconds. The Agera RS was powered by a twin turbocharged 5.0 liter V8 with 1,341 horsepower and 1,011 pound-feet of torque, and cost in the neighborhood of $2 million.

Acceleration: 0–60mph 2.8 seconds

Torque: 944 lb-ft

Power output: 960hp

Production years: 2015–2018

Production numbers: 27

Engine: 5.0 liter twin turbocharged V8

Weight: 3,075 lbs

Price: USD $2,500,000

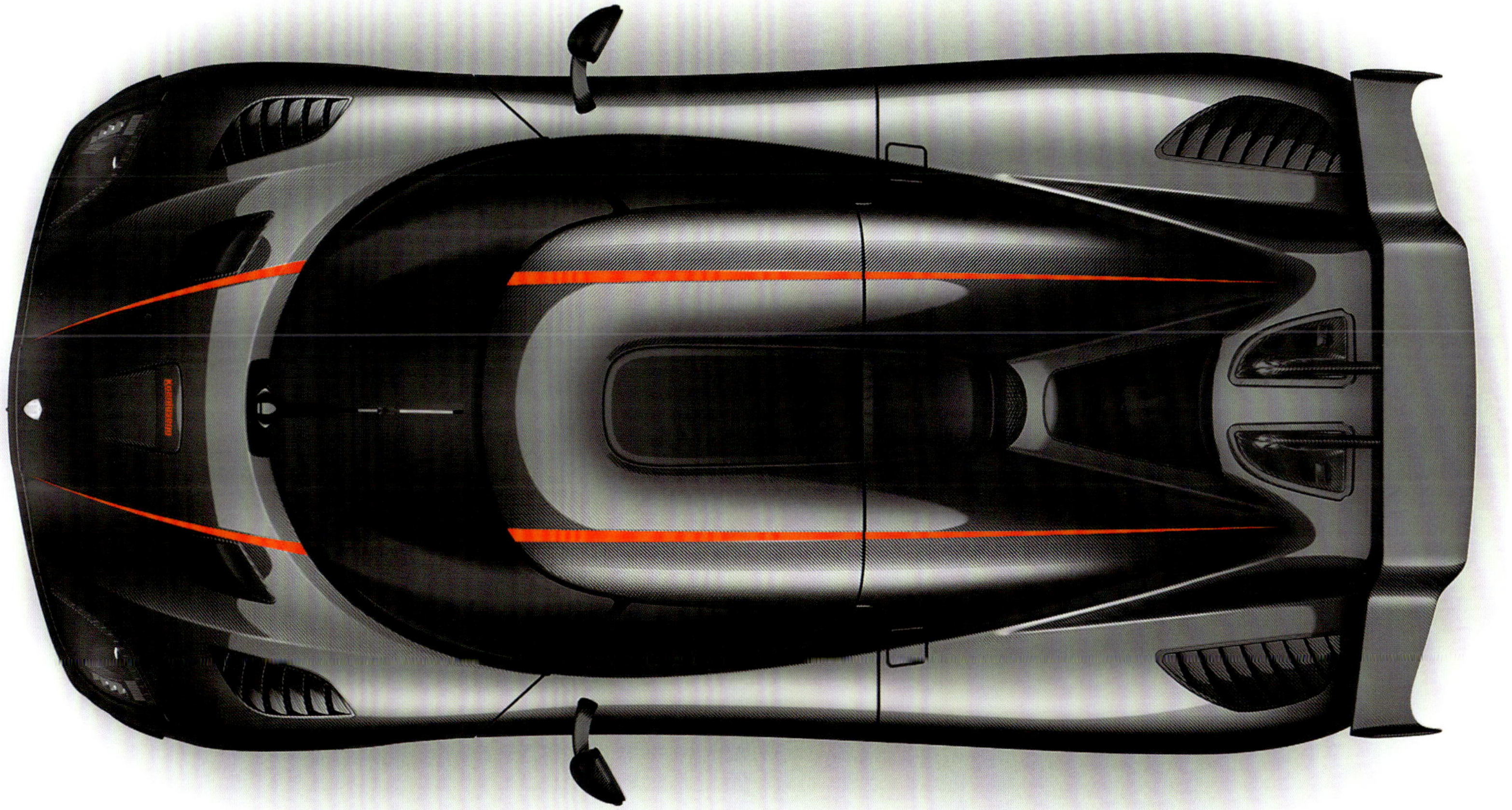

The Regera RS's exterior detail includes the double bubble roof, allowing better headroom. The raised sections of the roof are part of a continuing design element extending over the mid engine to the rear deck, with a clear pane set lower down the center.

KOENIGSEGG AUTOMOTIVE

Christian von Koenigsegg started his company in 1994, with the aim of producing hypercars that could compete with the best in the world on performance. Coming out of Sweden, he was only 22 years old when he made his intentions known to the public. It's remarkable that his first effort, the CC-V8, arrived by late 2001. Through gradual improvements, the company has gone from sourcing engines and operating systems from other companies, to building their own engines from the ground up.

Koenigsegg has never been a high-volume manufacturer, but has been a consistent player in the hypercar market. The company was also one of the first in the hypercar segment to begin working on alternative fuel engines. Even as larger companies make inroads in the segment, Koenigsegg has maintained its status as a solid and consistent competitor.

The interior keeps it simple and elegant. The center stack is dominated by rotary phone-style interior controls. The small inset screen sitting above was a standard of the era, featuring clean analog gauges and switches.

Koenigsegg CC850

In the hypercar business, anything approaching financial stability is worth celebrating. For Koenigsegg, the CC850 was the company's gift to itself and its founder. It celebrated both his 50th birthday and the 20th anniversary of the company's original CC8S. But the model's order books were filled so quickly that the company built an additional 20 units. This popularity emphasized the genuine warmth and loyalty of Koenigsegg's fans.

Mechanically, the CC850 is essentially a Jesko chassis with an exterior design that resembles the CC8S. The 5.0 liter twin turbo V8 produces 1,185hp through the dual clutch transmission. This model uses the Engage Shifter System, consisting of a clutch pedal and a shifter that has a traditional six-speed shifter gate. This allows the driver to decide between either automatic shifting or the old-school manual engagement of both the clutch and gear selection. This shifting option is unique in the industry.

The CC850 came as a targa top, allowing removal of the roof for open air motoring. As far as 1,150hp cars go, the specifications were geared towards touring rather than sport, and the model featured subtle bodywork and soft suspension settings. In many ways, the CC850 was a casual hypercar and a celebration of the company's two decades of existence in an industry where companies come and go.

Acceleration: 0–60 3.0 seconds

Torque: 1,020 lb-ft

Power output: 1,185hp

Production years: 2022–2023

Production numbers: 50, increased to 70

Engine: 5.0 liter twin turbo V8

Weight: 3,050 lbs

Price: USD $3,700,000

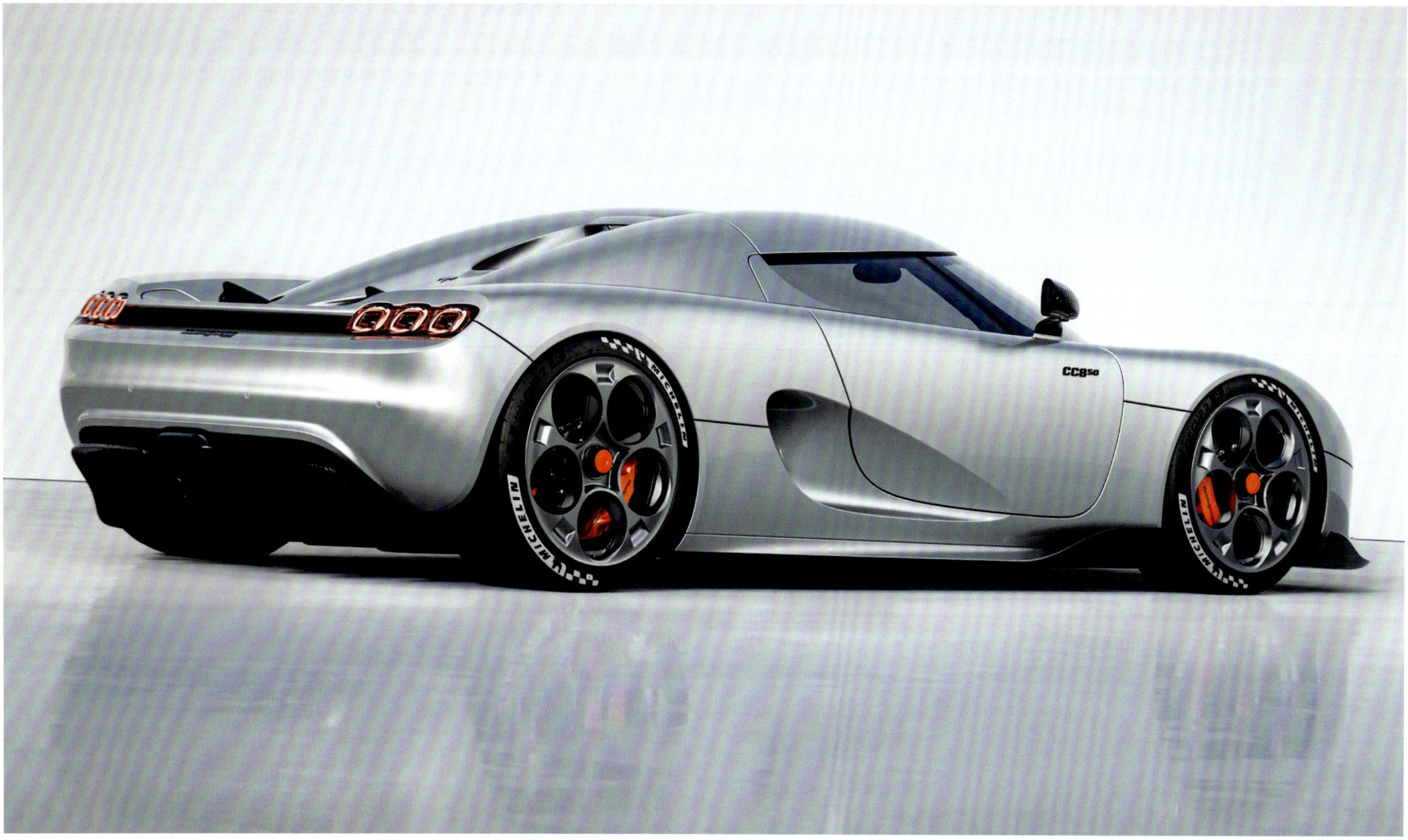
CC850
MICHELIN

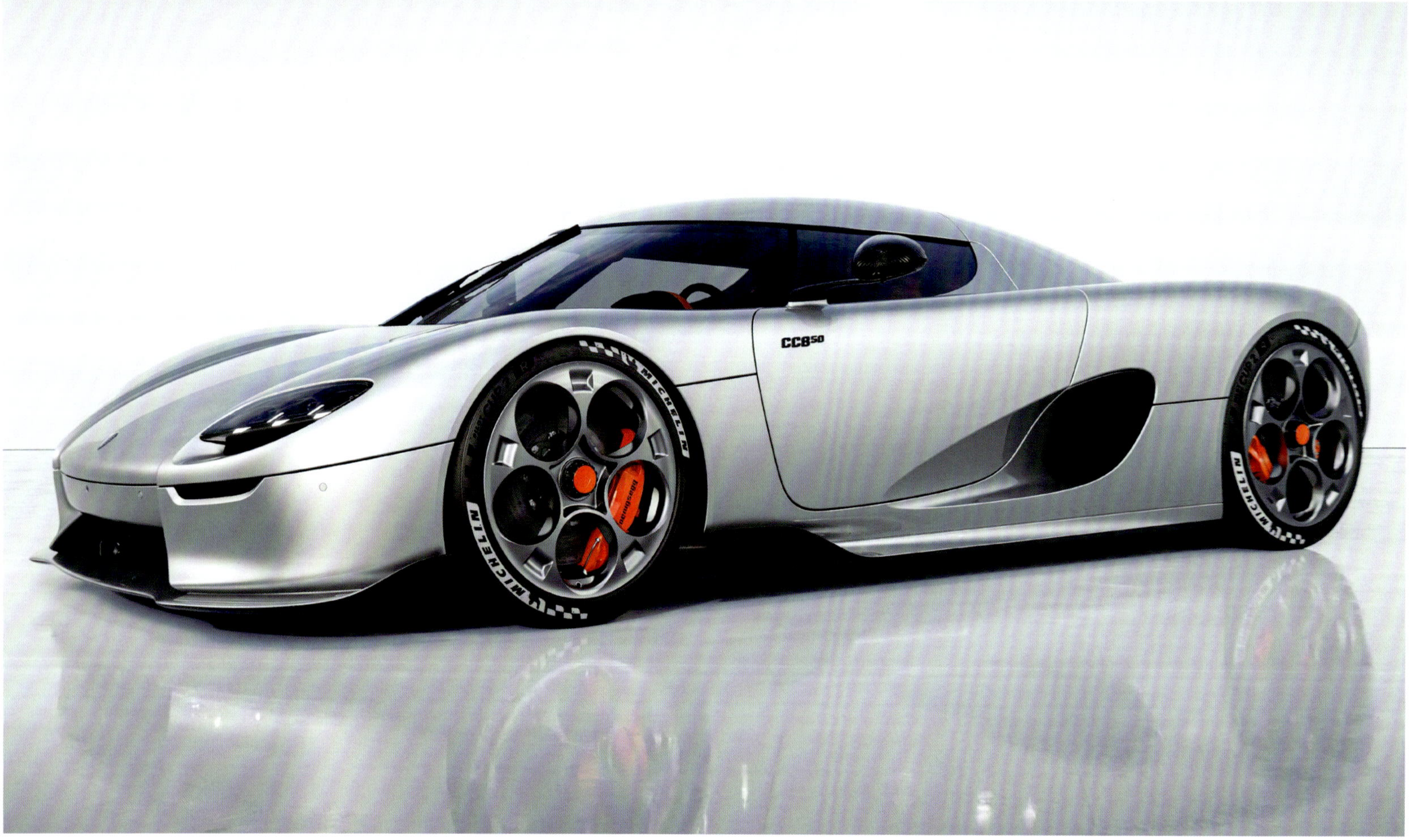
CC850
MICHELIN

KOENIGSEGG AUTOMOTIVE

The original twin turbo V8 in the CC8S was sourced from Ford. A perfect starting point for any hot rodder, the stout 5.0 liter responded well to strengthened internals and increased turbo boost to make big power reliably.

Once Koenigsegg had a little momentum and some sales under its belt, it designed its own aluminum block 5.0 liter V8 using the Ford engine as a starting point. This engine provided larger water jackets for more efficient cooling, a more rigid design to withstand turbo boost, and aluminum four-valve cylinder heads for better breathing.

Designing a new and reliable combustion engine is a noteworthy accomplishment for a small company. As Koenigsegg has transitioned into alternative fuels and hybrid setups incorporating electric motors, the original engine continues to be the anchor point for all of their cars.

The gorgeous interior features a shifter for the manual transmission. But with the incredible Koenigsegg-designed Engage Shift Sytem (ESS), the driver can choose to shift manually or set the car in automatic and leave the clutch pedal alone.

Koenigsegg

Gemera

The Gemera was the first Koenigsegg to offer four-passenger seating. Somehow, it lost no performance in the process. A true hybrid system, the Gemera produces 2,300hp from its V8/electric motor combination, easily ignoring the extra weight from extending the length to accommodate four adults.

Style-wise, the Gemera retains the hypercar coupe profile you would expect from the company. The most dramatic aspect of the design might be the extra-long doors, which retain a smooth profile but allow easy entry. They use dihedral synchro-helix actuation, opening out and then up with special hinges. This type of door hinge seems to be popular even on cars with normally sized openings.

With the mass market turning to SUVs and upright boxes, the Gemera manages to be both a hypercar and also, in its own way, one of the most sensible transportation devices you could own. It is space-efficient and comfortable for four people and their luggage. The hybrid power rivals even the most efficient high-speed train running on time, and the beautiful design inside and out makes this a singular example of a hypercar that offers breathtaking fun for the whole family.

Acceleration: 0–60mph 1.8 seconds

Torque: 2,028 lb-ft

Power output: 2,300hp

Production years: 2024–2025

Engine: 5.0 liter twin turbo V8, front axle-mount electric motor

Weight: 4,383 lbs

Price: USD $1,700,000

This image captures the audacity of the Gemera's impossibly long doors. But the design audacity does have a practical side—it allows an ease of entry that makes the four seats accessible in a way no other door design could.

KOENIGSEGG AUTOMOTIVE

Among the bigger hypercar manufacturers, none have resisted the lure of the sports SUV. And if the goal of a business is profit, why would they? But Koenigsegg's decision to make a proper four-seat, two-door coupe with hybrid drivetrain stands out as a true chart-your-own-course decision in the hypercar market. Originally, the Gemera plan involved a new, highly efficient three-cylinder combustion engine along with three smaller electric motors, all adding up to power figures similar to what the company twin turbo V8 supplied on its own. But preproduction, when the engine wasn't as good as hoped and other electric options were available, Koenigsegg changed direction. The electric power changed from three small motors to one large, 800hp electric motor, which was then coupled with the TT V8 to achieve the huge power gain. Not a bad way to solve a problem—and typical of the company's problem-solving adaptability.

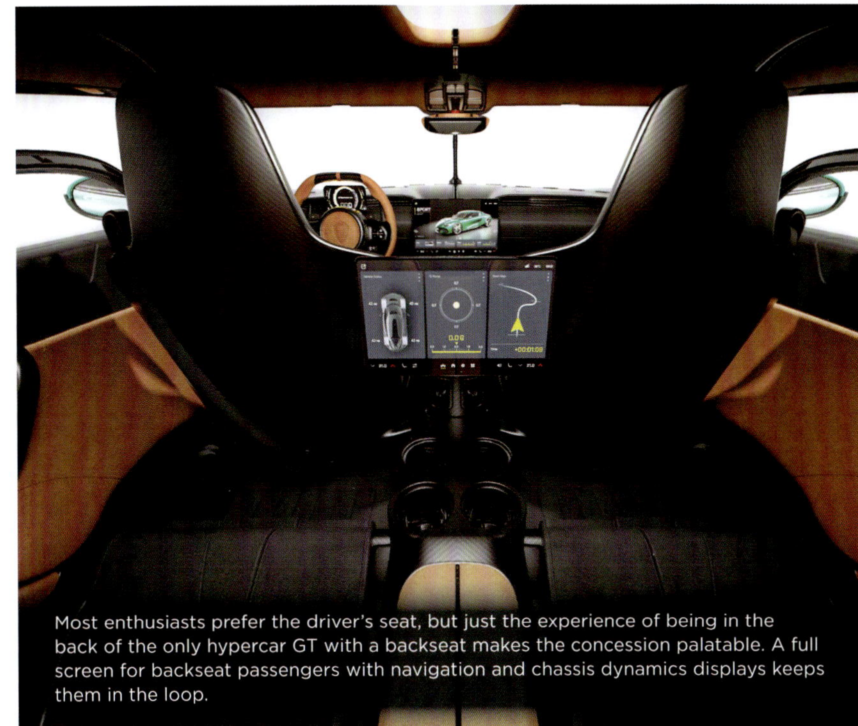

Most enthusiasts prefer the driver's seat, but just the experience of being in the back of the only hypercar GT with a backseat makes the concession palatable. A full screen for backseat passengers with navigation and chassis dynamics displays keeps them in the loop.

Koenigsegg
Jesko

Acceleration: 0–60mph 2.5 seconds

Torque: 738 lb-ft

Power output: 1,280hp (gasoline), 1,600hp (E85)

Production years: 2023–2024

Production numbers: est. 125

Engine: 5.0 liter, twin turbo V8

Weight: 3,131 lbs

Price: USD $3,000,000

The Jesko is the latest—and perhaps the last—model by Koenigsegg to rely only on their 5.0 liter V8 twin turbo motor. The Jesko comes in a "regular" track-oriented trim called the "Attack," and a lightweight hardcore version called the "Absolut."

The Jesko is a flexible-fuel hypercar. It is capable of running E85, an 85% ethanol fuel. This fuel is not only more thermally efficient, but also reduces harmful emissions. The reason that E85 is so popular with racing teams and owners of modified cars becomes apparent when looking at the power figures. On regular gasoline, Koenigsegg's excellent twin turbo V8 produces 1,280hp, the normal superlative output for this engine. But when running on E85, that power figure jumps to a scarcely believable 1,600hp.

The Jesko benefits from the engineering prowess of the company in many ways. Another unique detail is the in-house transmission, designated the Light Speed Transmission.

Technically, most transmissions switch gears by disengaging one gear and switching to another. Dual clutch transmissions make the change more quickly by allowing the transmission to preselect the next gear. But the LST improves on that by having all nine gears in constant rotation, with individual clutches that engage as needed, meaning there is essentially no changing of gears, only the different clutches engaging as the gear is selected. This brings the shift speed down to 2 milliseconds or even less, making the power delivery seamless.

Technical details aside, the main point about the transmission is that while other small companies find purchasing existing drivetrains to be expedient, Koenigsegg not only builds these things for themselves, but also has introduced new technology from a fresh perspective. The results have impressed both customers and other manufacturers.

The Jesko wears its downforce aero details proudly. The dive planes are in place as expected, but even by modern standards the bi-plane reverse-rake rear wing is dramatic. The Jesko also features the company's Autoskin system, where every panel can be opened electro-hydraulically.

KOENIGSEGG AUTOMOTIVE

As Koenigsegg looks towards the future, the Jesko represents a pivotal moment. The gasoline engine that Koenigsegg built has powered their hypercars in various states of tune for nearly 15 years, while the Gemera's 800hp electric motor proves they are ready for the future, whatever regulations may come their way.

This is where small, independent, engineering-driven companies like Koenigsegg are in a great position. They can adapt to rapid market changes without being tied up in long-term product planning. Larger companies do not have this nimble mobility. This is particularly important right now, as the move towards full, regulated electrification begins to appear premature, resulting in bigger companies having to scramble to modify timelines set a few years ago. In short, Koenigsegg is prepared for many possibilities in the changing energy landscape. Whether the trend is gas, electric, or multiple hybrid options, this is a company that can adapt rapidly.

Lamborghini Countach LPI 800-4

With any iconic nameplate in the automotive world, there are responsibilities and there are expectations. When a company is fortunate enough to have a nameplate that is the definition of an icon, that name must be handled with care. If a new version of the icon is adorned with that name, it needs to measure up. So it is with Lamborghini's Countach.

While it isn't the first hypercar in automotive history, in many ways it set the standard for what a hypercar is expected to look and sound like to this day. An impossibly sharp wedge when it debuted in 1974, it was a touchstone in the story of the hypercar. The Countach still informs opinions of how a hypercar should affect people visually.

So how does the 2022 tribute measure up? As it sits, the Aventador, on which the LPI 800-4 is based, already carried signature details that Lamborghini is known for, from the short and sharply sloped hood, to the cutout for the rear window nestled between the fenders. The lineage was clear.

The LPI-800-4 adds critical details that make it look like a natural progression from earlier models. For example, it has wheel arches in the fenders, a large NACA shaped duct on the sides, a glass roof treatment mimicking the earliest "Periscopio" versions of the original, and updated versions of the squared taillights set in the back. Power-wise, it is no slouch, taking the most powerful version of the Lamborghini V12 available and adding a supercapacitor that generates electric power. This adds 34hp to help mostly with torque fill at lower revs.

The end result has been admittedly polarizing among fans of the Countach. Some feel it isn't worthy of the original—including the designer of the original, Marcello Gandini—while others feel it isn't trying to be the original, but is merely paying respect and enhancing how connected they are. Context is everything, but ultimately, the LPI-800-4 is a worthy hypercar. It does what the big Lamborghini designs have always done best: provoke strong emotions.

Acceleration: 0–60mph 2.6 seconds

Torque: 557 lb-ft

Power output: 803hp combined

Production years: 2022

Production numbers: 112

Engine: 6.5 liter V12; front axle-mount electric motor

Weight: 3,515 lbs

Price: USD $2,640,000

LAMBORGHINI AUTOMOTIVE

If Ferrari is the standard, then Lamborghini is there to break the standard. This has been true since the company's inception. Company founder Ferruccio Lamborghini, who was famously insulted by Enzo Ferrari's casually condescending response to Ferruccio's issues with the clutch on his personal Ferrari, wanted to prove that it wasn't his inability to drive that was the source of the issue. Lamborghini then did something extraordinary: he built something better to prove Enzo wrong. This competitive spirit saw Lamborghini make cars not for racing, but for the street. Lamborghini felt that Ferrari's road car manufacturing was sloppy—simply a way to make money for its racing concern.

While the Countach is the hypercar wedge we all know and love, it was its predecessor, the Miura, that put Lamborghini front and center in the car community. It was also a true hypercar: gorgeous, fast, and excellent enough to force Ferrari to acknowledge Lamborghini as a worthy competitor.

The Aventador inspiration shows most clearly in the modern rocket-launcher style start button with red flip-up cover for full dramatic effect, along with centralized switchgear with an LCD display.

Lamborghini

Huracán STO

While the big V12 Lamborghinis always garner admiration, a smaller model in the lineup has often been just as wild and fast. When the Volkswagen Audi Group bought Lamborghini in the fall of 1998, the Diablo already existed—and not much else. They arrived just in time to fund proper engineering for the new Murcielago. Via platform sharing with Audi, they created the V10 Gallardo as an “entry level” Lamborghini—a car with both the proper looks and drivetrain worthy of the brand.

The follow up was the Huracán, and it has been a hit with fans since its debut in 2014. With that success came many new versions. The STO specification of the Huracán is the best interpretation of the hypercar ideal because it's not just an appearance package—though that is definitely a part of the equation for the STO—but because the STO is demonstrably different from the standard car.

The biggest change is in the drive system. Power is routed only to the rear wheels instead of four. This saves weight and contributes to a livelier and easier feel. The model uses carbon fiber for body panels, has less sound deadening, and features carbon bucket racing seats. The detail changes result in a drop of 200 pounds from the curb weight of a standard Huracán.

Acceleration: 0–60mph 2.8 seconds

Torque: 442 lb-ft

Power output: 630hp

Production years: 2021–2024

Production numbers: limited to 700

Engine: 5.2 liter V10

Weight: 3,172 lbs

Price: USD $344,000

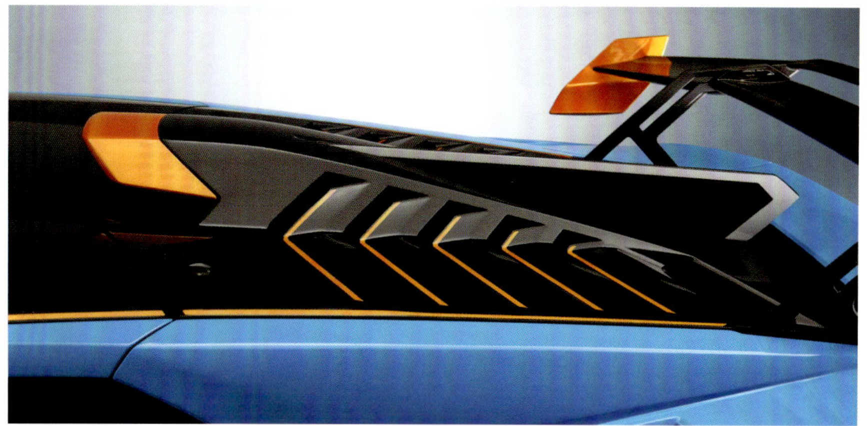

STO

LAMBORGHINI AUTOMOTIVE

The Huracán's successor, the Tememario, has made the change to hybrid power. The V10 is going away, to be replaced by a twin turbo V8 with three electric motors. This makes the Huracán's naturally aspirated rear-wheel drive setup appear resolutely old school.

But one of the charms of Lamborghini's cars, as dramatic as they've always looked, has been their straightforward approach to propulsion. This has traditionally meant bigger, naturally aspirated motors in flying wedges with a certain special look and feel.

Today's regulations about emissions and fuel efficiency make both the smaller turbo engines and electric motors in the Tememario a necessary and logical progression. From a performance perspective, this has not been a problem, as speed has continued to increase. Lamborghini also continues to successfully cultivate a high level of driver involvement. But as impressive as the new hypercars can be, one of the values of the STO going forward may be its simplicity.

The focused nature of the STO is evident in the interior. It features competition-spec bucket seats with full racing harnesses to keep occupants in place, along with grippy alcantara fabric for both the seats and the steering wheel.

Lamborghini

Revuelto

As with the Tememario and Huracán, the Revuelto was inspired by its predecessor, the Aventador. The Aventador was a relatively simple build. But tightening regulations and inherent power restrictions meant that the Revuelto would need a strategic rethink.

The Revuelto used an all-new V12. The decision to leave it naturally aspirated seems fitting, allowing for classic Lamborghini driving dynamics. The addition of electric motors to the V12 in the Revuelto was something of a foregone conclusion. Thanks to many of the company's models offering various hybrid drivetrains throughout the 2010s, Lamborghini had worked its way up to the Revuelto's specification gradually. From those different combinations, the choice for the Revuelto was three electric motors assisting the 814hp V12. For the first time, Lamborghini went the plug-in hybrid route. The Revuelto is capable of running on electric only propulsion (though only briefly, for about 5 miles).

Combined with the V12, the three electric motors bring the power up to 1,001hp—an incredibly high number. Nonetheless, four-digit power numbers are practically the norm at this point for legitimate players in the hypercar arena. The Lamborghini lineage is very clear both inside and out.

Acceleration: 0–60mph 2.3 seconds

Torque: 783 lb-ft combined

Power output: 1,001hp combined

Production years: 2024 and beyond

Engine: 6.5 liter V12, 3 AC electric motors

Weight: 4,450 lbs

Price: USD $608,360

The Revuelto's nose features the new light signature standard for Lamborghini design: arrows pointed towards the center. Along the side, air intakes stand out proudly from the body from top to bottom, allowing the hybrid V12 to take in the copious amount of air it needs to breathe.

LAMBORGHINI AUTOMOTIVE

For Lamborghini, design language is critical when updating its flagship models. Beginning with the Countach, the company has always found a way to tie the design of one model to another. Given how recognizable Lamborghini's models are, giving nods to existing lineages is smart business.

As impressive as the 1,001hp hypercar is, we know there is room for improvement. With electric motors comes more modular capability, and this may be expanded upon in the future. Electric motors can be replaced with more powerful units without requiring extensive reengineering or chassis modifications. Even the new V12 can probably be massaged for more power as new trim levels are produced, meaning that this Revuelto may be the basis for new models for years to come.

Lamborghini Sian

The Sian was introduced to the public before the Reveuelto as the first hybrid created by Lamborghini. Based on the Aventador chassis, the Sian had the V12, but included a supercapacitor mounted to the transmission for an extra 34hp.

As the V12 produces 774hp already, the extra 34hp doesn't make a big difference. But it's not about how much, but when. In this case, the answer is instantly, helping low rpm power and smoothing out acceleration from rest.

The Sian's development was always about design. As a first foray into hybrid power, Lamborghini wanted to offer a limited-run hypercar (just 82 examples total) that would give a glimpse into the future both visually and mechanically. Beginning with the Y-shaped driving lights, the front end provided a glimpse into the future. At the same time, key visual clues from the Countach were employed, including square lights for the rear, a Periscopio rear view window, and a cutout in the roof to allow (some) visibility to the back.

The Sian has set a standard for the next generation of Lamborghini hypercars. As other manufacturers observed, Lamborghini noted a fervent desire from their most loyal customers for something very exclusive. The Sian delivered.

Acceleration: 0–60mph 2.9 seconds

Torque: 561 lb-ft

Power output: 808hp combined

Production years: 2020–2022

Production numbers: 82

Engine: 6.5 liter V12, 1 supercapacitor

Weight: 3,350 lbs

Price: USD $3,000,000

As dramatic as the Sian coupe is, the Roadster's design details steal the show. With the roof removed, the roll hoops are matched by the engine cover design with the inset down the middle, creating a center tunnel—a signature V12 Lamborghini design since the Countach.

LAMBORGHINI AUTOMOTIVE

The Sian was one of a string of successful limited specials from Lamborghini through the 2010s. Like many of the other established manufacturers in the hypercar space, they saw a demand for something that went beyond what was already considered extreme. What's fascinating is how, even as the number of manufacturers in the hypercar market increases, the demand has not abated. More and more players come in the arena, and in some cases field multiple models at the same time.

Lamborghini Veneno

Thanks to Lamborghini's continued success, the company made a foray into the realm of limited production specials: the Veneno. Released as a celebration of the company's 50th anniversary, nothing about the car was restrained. Lamborghini rather cautiously planned a run of only 14 units. The Veneno's origins are with the Aventador. While the Lamborghini bloodlines are clearly laid over a tight cockpit and full downforce aerodynamic trim, the model also bears more than just a passing resemblance to IMSA and Le Mans race cars. Airflow management is highlighted by the inclusion of a rear "dorsal fin" bisecting the engine cover.

Power came from the most powerful version of the Aventador's V12, a 750hp engine aided by a more extensive use of carbon fiber that dropped the curb weight to under 3,300 pounds. The interior made extensive use of Alcantara and the race bucket seats emphasized the simple purpose of the Veneno.

And talk about exclusive—even by hypercar standards, the 14-car run was small. Eleven were roadsters and just three were coupes, all of them spoken for before production ever began. And with a price starting at $4,000,000, Lamborghini found that its niche cars were worth the time and effort it took to produce them.

Acceleration: 0–60mph 2.8 seconds

Torque: 507 lb-ft

Power output: 750hp

Production years: 2013–2014

Production numbers: 14

Engine: 6.5 liter V12

Weight: 3,278 lbs

Price: USD $4,000,000

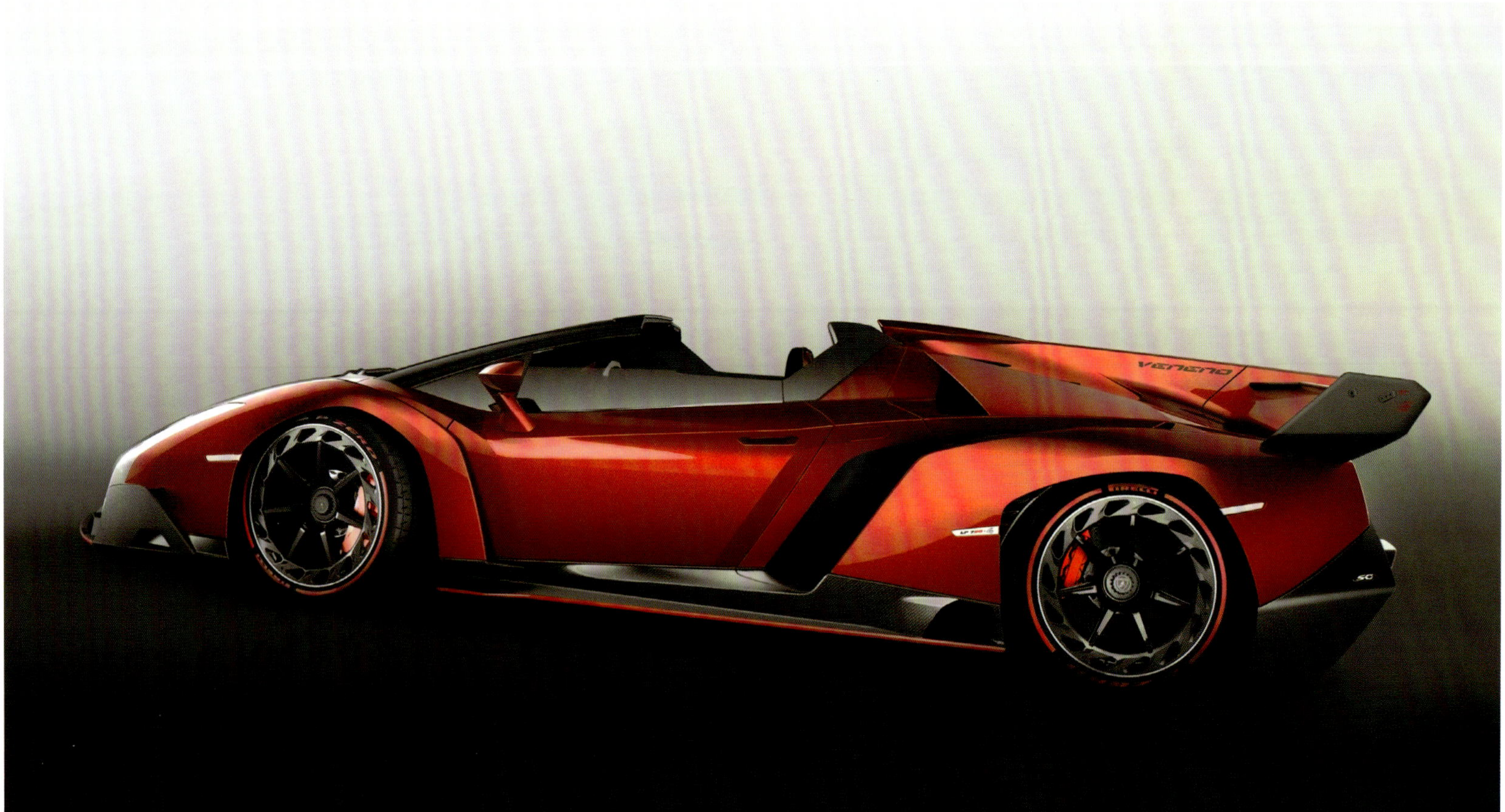

With or without a roof, the dorsal fin in the center of the back deck of the Veneno stands out. Ostensibly for better stability as seen on Le Mans Prototype racers, its presence is noticeable even with the dramatic details surrounding it.

LAMBORGHINI AUTOMOTIVE

Lamborghini is known for provocative designs and overall trendsetting. Yet in many ways, especially under the wing of the VW Audi Group, the company's designs would be better described as restrained and cohesive. But the Veneno's design broke through with an intentionally provocative and purposeful look. The intention to invoke prototype racers led to dorsal fins and elaborate rear diffusers. These, surprisingly, don't look integrated; in this case, design takes a back seat to effectiveness.

The overall effect is sharp. It still somehow looks like a Lamborghini and is visually effective. The model foreshadowed how future Lamborghini specials would be allowed a little freedom from the constraints placed on bigger production runs.

Lotus Evija

After decades of producing some of the smallest, lightest cars ever sold to the public, the latest iteration of this company has committed to electrification. Known primarily for Formula 1 and some of the smallest and lightest two-seater sports cars you could buy, Lotus has applied its know-how to a long and lean coupe that sports a healthy 2,021hp for motivation.

Lotus didn't intend the Evija to be an also-ran. The Evija's slick design is aided by active aero, with pronounced side intakes over a wasp-waisted form that makes for an intimate cockpit for the two occupants. Inside, the lean, clean design is meant to marry modern elements and tech to an airy greenhouse and low dashboard.

Technically, the emphasis is on driving dynamics. From the company's perspective, one of the most important things that will contribute to driver enjoyment is concentrating mass at the center of the vehicle. Many electric vehicles spread the batteries across the bottom, creating "skateboard" platforms, with the body sitting on top. But the Evija stacks the batteries directly behind the seats, thus concentrating the greatest weight in the middle of the car. This results in a pliant sports car that is much more willing to change direction.

One of the greatest small details about this old-school approach to driving fun is in the power steering, which uses hydraulics instead of an electric unit. It may not be as efficient, but for driving feel, it's worlds better and gives a more natural response. The car was completely sold out before any were delivered.

Acceleration: 0–60mph 2.9 seconds
Torque: 1,257 lb-ft
Power output: 2,021hp
Production years: 2023
Production numbers: limited to 130
Engine: 4 electric motors, hub mounted
Weight: 3,700 lbs
Price: USD $2,300,000

The exterior design echoes Lotus's most recent design details of the Elise, Exige and Evora, with a tight canopy for the passenger compartment. The larger overall size is still lithe and lean, evoking the diminutive sports cars Lotus is famous for.

LOTUS AUTOMOTIVE

For decades, the Lotus brand reflected the values of its founder, the late great Colin Chapman. Chapman was fully immersed in England's postwar racing world. He focused on both lightweight street cars and Formula 1. With his well-known mantra "just add lightness" informing everything he made, his cars were almost notorious for sacrificing durability in the name of shedding weight. That approach worked for his Formula 1 successes. His production cars were also praised by amateur racers all through the '60s and '70s. Lotus products shined wherever agility took emphasis over outright horsepower.

Even as the company experienced the usual financial ups and downs, it found great success with superlight cars like the Elise and Exiges, using light and reliable Toyotas and wrapping them in tight little coupe shapes. This brought affordable speed that had no equal among modern competition. Along the way, Lotus earned the undying loyalty of rabid enthusiasts.

Today Lotus continues to find success with its proven formula. With its solid track record and long history in racing, it's not surprising that Lotus has found an older, wealthier clientele already lined up and waiting to purchase its take on the hypercar.

Maserati GT2 Stradale

Maserati's MC20, the basis for the GT2 Stradale, proved that there was a market for the rather comfy Maserati hypercar. What should surprise nobody is that, while it succeeded at its mission, there were those who wanted a meaner version of the "nice" hypercar. Maserati didn't need much convincing as this was always in the plan. Hence the GT2 Stradale.

The MC20s started with an excellent platform and added a modest bump in power (641hp—a mere 21hp more). They took aim at a higher rpm range for a more exhilarating experience. To make the engine's life easier, the GT2 Stradale lost roughly 130 pounds and added more aggressive aero for stronger downforce at speed.

The exterior changes included a larger rear wing that can be adjusted manually, and a larger nose in front to allow increased airflow. The acceleration is impressive, especially given that it is only rear-wheel drive.

The overall effect is predictable: not as relaxed, stiffer and louder, but with appreciable differences in ability at speed. It's still a Grand Tourer, but aimed for the track day or a canyon-strafing blast instead of long-distance, high-speed touring. None of this should be a surprise; it's yet another example of a great adjustable platform meant to play its size advantage against bigger, heavier hypercars.

Acceleration: 0–60mph 2.8 seconds

Torque: 538 lb-ft

Power output: 631hp

Production years: starting in 2024

Engine: 3.0 liter twin turbo V6

Weight: 3,552 lbs

The details of the GT2 Stradale are exercises in visual aggression. The smooth contours of the MC20 give way to the vented hood and larger air intakes in the front fascia for better cooling and airflow, while also providing the downforce required of a more track-oriented specification.

MASERATI AUTOMOTIVE

The MC20 and the GT2 Stradale are great hypercars, and it can't be overemphasized how important they are for the company. Its luxury sedans and coupes see stiff competition in a crowded market, so it would be foolish of Maserati not to capitalize on its racing heritage to create a market advantage.

This section of the hypercar market continues to be extremely dynamic. With electrification comes the openings for upstarts. The evolving technology is an opportunity to think outside the box and innovate clean-sheet designs.

Still, experience is worth a lot. So when it comes to creating a gasoline-powered hypercar capable of great speed and handling, knowing the terrain and tapping that experience is a viable road to a great product. With continued success, Maserati should be able to keep its share of the market secure.

Maserati MC20

The MC20's interior is purposeful and clean, but entirely in keeping with the GT mission. The switchgear is another example of the current trend away from too many screen-accessed controls, with knobs and buttons that provide true tactile feedback in place of touch screens.

Acceleration: 0-60mph 3.2 seconds

Torque: 538 lb-ft

Power output: 621hp

Production years: 2022

Engine: 3.0 liter twin turbo V6

Weight: 3,757 lbs

Price: USD $216,000

The MC20 is Maserati's best case for the "practical" hypercar—a rapid conveyance restrained in looks and purpose that refrains from the more extroverted style of most cars in the class. It was a smart move on the part of Ferrari's sister company. While the Ferraris go for the extreme, the Maserati can comfortably sit in the "casual" hypercar slot and make a compelling case.

While sharing many aspects with similar engines by Ferrari and Alfa Romeo, the "Nettuno" V6 in the MC20 is mostly its own animal, with heads and induction unique to Maserati. The 621hp figure is relatively modest (but not by combustion motor standards, and especially not for a twin turbo V6). In the MC20's case, the emphasis on a GT approach makes for an incredible road car. Comfortable and rapid, the MC20 makes engagement a pleasure instead of an assault on the senses. This is not new in the exotic car world, but as hypercars have gotten increasingly capable, there are surprisingly few hypercars that aim to achieve speed with this kind of composure.

The exterior design of the MC20 ties in with its mission. Devoid of multiple angles and extravagantly large aero appendages, the design has curves and lines emphasizing looks over efficiency and downforce. So, as subtle hypercars go, the MC20 deserves the attention and praise it gets.

Smooth and gimmick-free, the MC20 is a refreshing exercise in restraint. While still sleek and equipped with butterfly dihedral doors, this Maserati avoids multiple lines and creases on the exterior, yet appears all the more dramatic in its purposeful minimalism.

MASERATI AUTOMOTIVE

The MC20 was Maserati's declaration of intent: it still meant to compete against the big boys. For the last twenty or thirty years, Maserati has relied heavily on both Fiat and Ferrari to keep it going. Having Ferrari as a source for engines, of course, is a great situation to be in. For the most part Maserati has stuck to GTs and sedans, but its racing heritage has informed even its regular sedans and coupes. Of course, those incredible Ferrari V8s never hurt either.

What really helped Maserati in modern times has been sharing the Ferrari Enzo platform to create the Maserati MC12. While it is subtly different and more GT-oriented, the direct tie-in to Ferrari has helped elevate the automaker in the public eye.

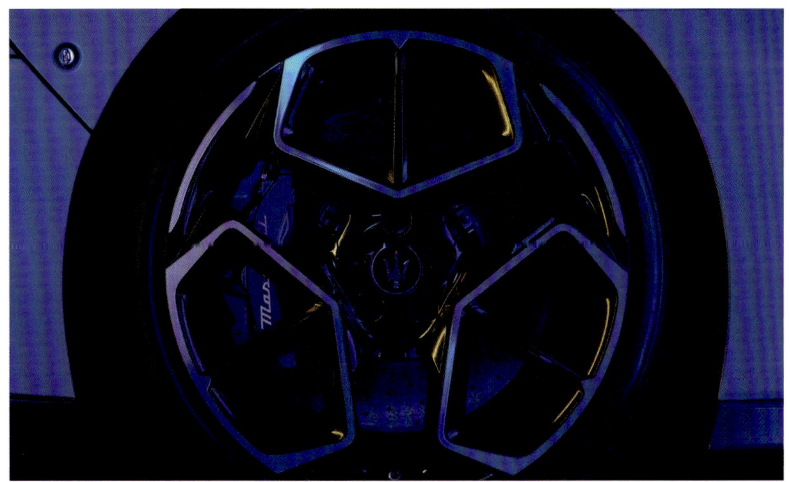

McLaren 765LT

The 765LT is one of the best versions of the modern "affordable" McLaren. The MP4-12C, introduced in 2011, was the first model by the modern McLaren company. With this machine, McLaren demonstrated how smooth and comfortable a rapid hypercar could be. With its fully linked hydraulic suspension, it stunned contemporary reviewers with its supple ride and "coddling," even as it out-hustled the competition in speed and pace.

The 765LT is the child of the 12C. It's just as comfortable as its forebear, but nothing short of vicious with its speed. While the 12C's 593hp is great, the jaw-dropping 755hp of the 765LT (so named for its European power rating) is very much next-level business. The 0–60 time of 2.7 seconds is especially impressive considering the fact that it's a rear-wheel-drive car. Once it hits 100mph, the grip means ferocious speed.

The engine is McLaren's own—a twin turbo V8 that the automaker uses in almost everything they've made since the 12C's introduction. While power has increased and acceleration is better than ever, the 765LT employs more downforce for stability than its predecessors. This means that its top speed of "only" 205mph is down from 212mph. But with contemporary tests achieving the quarter mile in under 10 seconds, the 765 remains one of the most rapid GT hypercars available. It maintains McLaren's reputation as the choice for those who don't believe in sacrificing comfort for speed.

Acceleration: 0–60mph 2.7 seconds

Torque: 590 lb-ft

Power output: 755hp

Production years: 2020–2023

Production numbers: 765

Engine: 4.0 liter twin turbo V8

Weight: 3,300 lbs

Price: USD $382,500

McLaren's signature headlights stand out from those of typical slant-nosed hypercars. Its aggressive surface detailing reflects the startling performance capacity of the LT series. Even more startling is that while some manufacturers seem to exaggerate their numbers, somehow this McLaren's 755hp rating feels modest.

MCLAREN AUTOMOTIVE

From its incredible motorsports history to its standing as the manufacturer of arguably the best hypercar of all time, McLaren's pedigree is in no doubt. Starting with the namesake Bruce McLaren, the company produced some of the most dominant race cars of all time, from road racing legends to the stunning Honda-powered Formula 1 cars piloted by the likes of Ayrton Senna and Alain Prost.

Any conversation about McLaren street cars has to include the F1. The Gordon Murray-designed, ground-up clean slate design featured the 627hp BMW V12. It was the first McLaren to employ the iconic three-person seating with the driver's seat in the center. That car is still highly prized. Only 106 were produced from 1992 to 2000, and the model now commands a minimum USD $20,000,000. The new McLaren hypercars are produced in larger numbers and aren't derived from the F1, but the company has done an incredible job following in its own footsteps, producing incredible street cars that loyal fans always snatch up.

McLaren Elva

For many owners, the beauty of the modern McLaren lies in its combination of speed and tranquility. It's the quintessential GT experience of comfort paired with rapid pace. The Elva, in contrast, increases the pace, and throws the tranquility into the rushing air.

Among hypercars, there are many manufacturers offering models that lack a roof. But the sunny-days-only Elva is the rarest of the rare: It does away with the windshield. The Elva is an incredible hypercar, inspired by the windshield-free racecars built for McLaren in the 1960s. As a special version of the McLaren platform, the Elva is wonderfully radical and committed to fun driving. Power from the company's 4.0 twin turbo V8 is increased to 804hp, while weight is dropped by a solid 400 pounds to make for a super lean hypercar.

Windflow management, always important for hypercars, is crucial in a design like this. To minimize buffeting, McLaren created a system it terms the Active Air Management System (AAMS). This includes a spoiler that is speed activated in front of the passenger compartment. This keeps the airstream flowing up and over the heads of occupants without interfering with the forward view. The interior is suitably minimalist, but the center console design emphasizes the space between the driver and passenger, with the race buckets looking more like separate pods for the people inside.

The Elva does have two options: an audio system and an optional short windscreen if a customer decides these are necessary. But the Elva seems like the best expression of the hypercar ethos on the cutting edge. It is absolutely committed to speed and even considers glass optional.

Acceleration: 0-60mph 2.6 seconds

Torque: 590 lb-ft

Power output: 804hp

Production years: 2020

Production numbers: 149

Engine: 4.0 liter twin turbo V8

Weight: 2,798 lbs

Price: USD $1,695,000

There are convertibles, there are removable targa tops, and then there's the Elva. Providing a fully visceral experience, the Elva turns a wind in your hair experience into something more like riding a motorcycle. Leaning into the wind, deflector or no, is a different level of driver (and passenger) involvement.

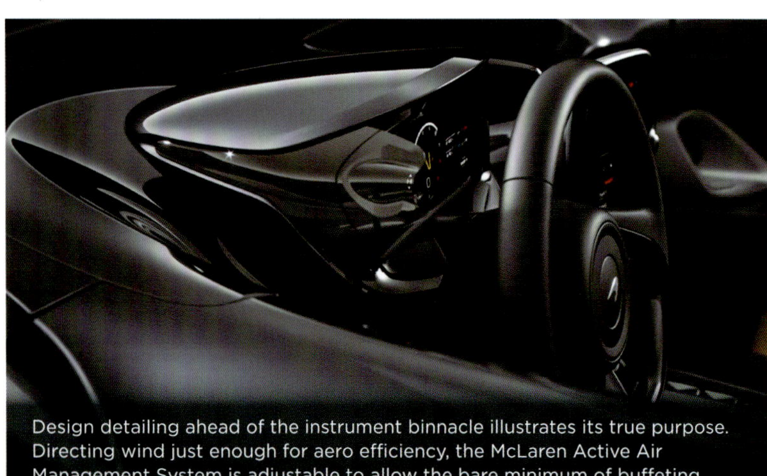

Design detailing ahead of the instrument binnacle illustrates its true purpose. Directing wind just enough for aero efficiency, the McLaren Active Air Management System is adjustable to allow the bare minimum of buffeting reduction for the cockpit. Some of that rush of air is the idea with this design.

MCLAREN AUTOMOTIVE

McLaren's racing roots can often be found in its product engineering decisions. Its current products have definitely been shining examples of good engineering. The immensely impressive hydraulic suspension system comes to mind. Marketing doesn't hurt, but the inherent excellence of the chassis has proven itself over time.

The great thing about the hypercar market is that it allows whimsy and fun. It's an exclusive niche for hardcore enthusiasts, many of whom want something completely novel out of these super-expensive models. A model like the Elva can only exist because the market exists. It is truly a niche offering and yet a popular one—the Elva sold out as soon as it was offered. This is good news because for a long time McLaren was operating on a tight budget. Being able to repurpose its platforms for variations like this works in its favor.

McLaren

P1

McLaren released the P1 as a flagship model from what it called its Ultimate Series, a step above the line that produced the MP4-12C and its offspring like the 765LT. The P1 was positioned as the brand's successor to the mighty F1, but even more powerful and exclusive.

The P1 was McLaren's first entry into the hybrid hypercar segment. Coming along in the same era as Porsche's 918 Spyder and the Ferrari LaFerrari, it was at the forefront of hybrid utilization at the high end, finding ways to use electrification not for better fuel mileage, but for performance. The instant response of the electric motor meant it had noticeable impact on low-speed power, moving from a stop, or coming out of a corner going full throttle.

The hybrid drivetrain produced a noteworthy 903hp. Also noteworthy: the curb weight of under 3,100 pounds undercut the 918 Spider and La Ferrari by hundreds of pounds. Rear drive only meant the P1 didn't have the grip off the line like its competitors, but the P1 had the typically wicked rolling acceleration that McLaren products have been known for. The light weight was what made the P1 such a hit with enthusiasts. At the time of the model's introduction, McLaren stated that the intent was not to be the fastest hypercar in a straight line, but to be the most rewarding track and enthusiast driving option. There seemed to be an implicit acknowledgement that the P1 wasn't going to out-accelerate a Veyron in a straight line. The point was that any road circuit would find the Veyron out-hustled by the light, lithe P1. By any standard, the P1 fulfills the mission.

Acceleration: 0–60mph 2.7 seconds

Torque: 664 lb-ft

Power output: 903hp combined

Production years: 2013–2015

Production numbers: 375

Engine: 3.8 liter twin turbo V8, 1 AC electric motor

Weight: 3,075 lbs

Price: USD $1,150,000

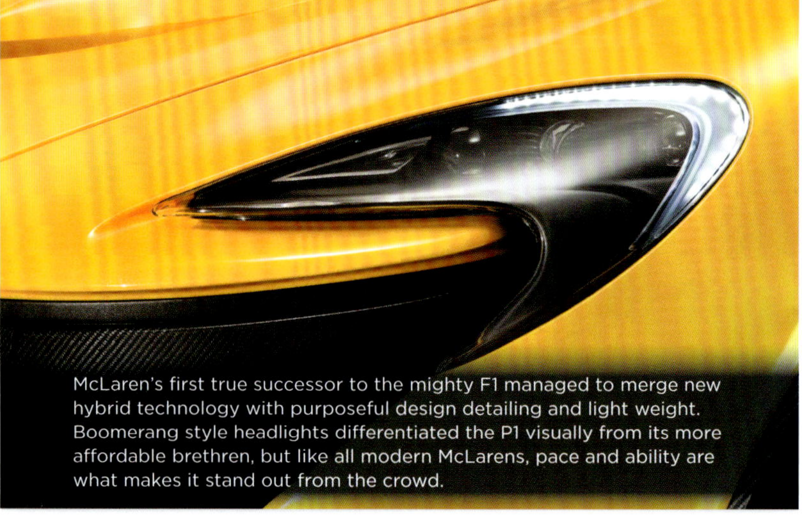

McLaren's first true successor to the mighty F1 managed to merge new hybrid technology with purposeful design detailing and light weight. Boomerang style headlights differentiated the P1 visually from its more affordable brethren, but like all modern McLarens, pace and ability are what makes it stand out from the crowd.

MCLAREN AUTOMOTIVE

Connecting hybrid hypercars with racing technology was intuitive for McLaren. As Formula 1 racing began adopting electrification for the series, manufacturers leaped to adopt the new paradigm. The P1 adhered to a simple form of hybridization. There was no plug-in capability, no electric-only mode, and one electric motor meant to assist. It was around this time that the term "torque-fill" began to appear. Between turbos and dual clutch semi-automatic transmissions, electric motors were coming to be relied on to get vehicles moving from a stop. One result of this has been a reduction in the jerkiness that can occur as the clutches engage. The latest hybrid systems are offering electric only modes more frequently. These are still usually only for a few miles. As one of the first such systems, the P1 benefits from not relying heavily on the hybrid mode and feeling dated as a result.

McLaren

The McLaren Senna was a testament to the company's racing heritage. Founder Bruce McLaren was a New Zealand-born driver who started building English race cars in 1963. Legendary Brazilian driver Ayrton Senna raced for McLaren from 1988 to 1993, racking up three Formula 1 world championships. He was tragically killed while driving for another team in 1994.

The McLaren Senna was built as an uncompromising track car that could set fast lap times, yet was street legal. The Senna was based on the 720S. While the 720S was comfortable and docile for a mid-engine supercar, the track-focused Senna had firmer suspension and lacked sound insulation. All unnecessary weight was eliminated. The 2,641-pound car was powered by a 789hp, twin turbocharged 4.0 liter V8 and was capable of a top speed of 208mph. Acceleration times were: 0-62mph in 2.8 seconds, 0-124mph in 6.8 seconds, and 0-186mph in 17.5 seconds. Strong brakes are important to quick lap times and the Senna could come to a complete stop from 62mph in less than 100 feet. Each carbon-ceramic brake disc took seven months to create.

The Senna's aggressive styling was an exercise in "form follows function" with an emphasis on generating downforce to keep the car stable at high speeds. McLaren claimed the Senna generated 1,763 pounds of downforce at 155mph. The cost of the Senna was around $1 million, but the 500-car quota was sold out before production began.

Acceleration: 0-60mph 2.8 seconds

Torque: 590 lb-ft

Power output: 789hp

Production years: 2018–2021

Production numbers: 500

Engine: 4.0 liter twin turbo V8

Weight: 2,641 lbs

Price: USD $1,000,000

The Senna has features one would expect from a car named after one of the best F1 drivers in history. Some of the amazing additional details like windows in the lower door skin are there simply because McLaren wanted them to be there.

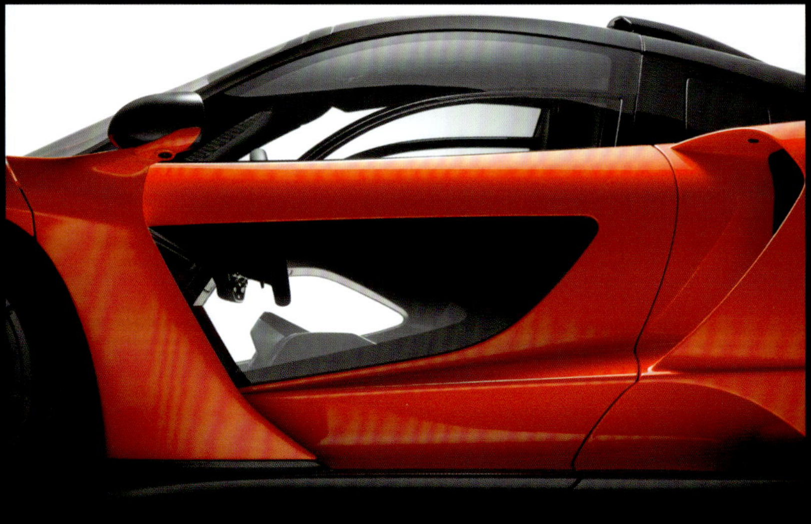

MCLAREN AUTOMOTIVE

Using the "Senna" name comes with great responsibility. Ayrton Senna's passing was devastating to his fans, especially in his home country of Brazil. In that country he was practically worshipped. Videos of his exploits as a driver for the McLaren team are still breathtaking. Tarnishing his memory would be an unforgivable offense.

McLaren knew its mission. The Senna is a driver's car first and foremost. Given its namesake, it made sense to give this model a large complement of active aero and back that up with exacting weight saving measures to maximize power.

The continued success of McLaren in Formula 1 makes future model tie-ins likely. What especially guarantees their future success are the continual core mechanical improvements, regardless of what new trim and colors are trotted out.

McLaren Solus GT

In the 2010s, McLaren had seen the same success with responses to its hypercars that other manufacturers were enjoying. So by 2020, it seemed likely that they would eventually make a truly dedicated track-only machine, using the available factory mechanicals to full effect.

That didn't quite prepare the public for the Solus GT. Truly bespoke, McLaren made a hypercar with some unique properties. It was built from the ground up and had a production run of only 25. Starting with the chassis, McLaren chose not to base the Solus on street cars, but instead developed a modified carbon-fiber monocoque based on proven Formula 1 experience. In fact, most of its construction parameters can withstand race-pace crash forces. The driver compartment is accessed not by doors, but via a sliding canopy top for maximum rigidity. The driver compartment is equipped with just one seat—no passengers allowed.

The engine is the biggest surprise. It is not based on the V6 or V8 engines used in street cars, but instead has a wild, freshly designed and naturally aspirated V10. Derived from a Judd racing engine but new for McLaren, it produces 829hp while redlining at 10,000 rpm.

As a one-seater, the Solus GT is extreme even by track-only hypercar standards, but for 25 lucky customers, it's another breathtaking special from a company that knows how to build them.

Acceleration: 0–60mph 2.6 seconds

Torque: 479 lb-ft

Power output: 829hp

Production years: 2023

Production numbers: 25

Engine: 5.2 liter V10

Weight: 2,205 lbs

Price: est. USD $3,000,000

The McLaren F1 monocoque is the basis for the Solus's design details. That includes the sliding canopy for entry, and a minimum concession to road use. The exterior shape evokes Le Mans Prototype elements, and the single seater cockpit does away with anything not necessary for rapid driving.

MCLAREN AUTOMOTIVE

No hypercar builder needs an excuse to build a racing car. But given the extent of their F1 racing history (second in age only to Ferrari), it makes sense that McLaren has succeeded easily in building a competitive track-ready hypercar. The Solus GT isn't just interesting in its own right; given the shape and style of it, one can't help but wonder how well suited it might be for existing series like Le Mans or IMSA. While there are no official plans, McLaren's road car division was just purchased by a company that promises to increase funding for research and development. Given that, it will be interesting to see what other avenues McLaren could take going forward.

McLaren Speedtail

Acceleration: 0–60mph 2.8 seconds

Torque: 848 lb-ft combined

Power output: 1,035hp combined

Production years: 2020

Production numbers: 106

Engine: 4.0 liter twin turbo V8, 1 AC electric motor

Weight: 3,305 lbs

Price: USD $2,000,000

McLaren's exterior designs have always been purposeful. Lean and tight lines have long been the norm. The company eschews the dramatic and overt style of the Italians in favor of details that emphasize form following function.

That philosophy holds true for the Speedtail. Its design focuses on optimized aerodynamics and maximum speed. Nonetheless, McLaren managed to create one of the most voluptuous and striking shapes in their history.

The design brief was clear. Utilize the best available hybrid drivetrain for power, then use active aero and a teardrop shape to upset the wind as minimally as possible. The name of the model highlights the most dramatic aspect. The extended tail is what makes the shape so slippery. It functions to extend and smooth the airflow behind the car, making the 250mph top speed a relatively easy achievement.

Other aero details are easily spotted. The aero discs on the front wheels evoke dedicated Bonneville racers. Exterior mirrors were eliminated and replaced with small rear facing cameras. Their video displays rest on both A-pillars. This tweak makes a significant difference in the streamlining process.

Inside, the lean look continues, with the signature center driver position revealing McLaren DNA. The two passenger seats on either side evoke the McLaren F1. The primary controls located above the driver emphasize the cockpit feel of the interior.

The original McLaren F1 street car was a classic Gordon Murray exercise in design restraint. The headline for this model might be its center driving seat position (with the two passenger seats set back and to the sides).

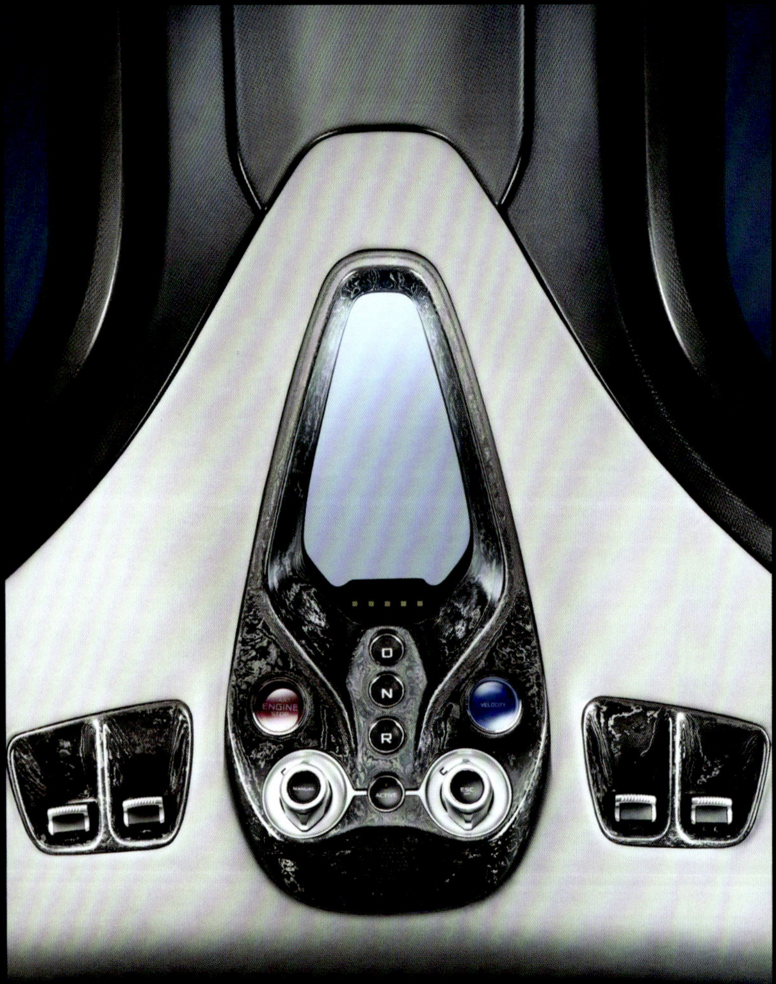

MCLAREN AUTOMOTIVE

As a performance target, even many decades on, the original McLaren F1 is formidable. The Speedtail is the first street McLaren to top the F1's 241mph. Not only is it higher, but it's significantly quicker getting to that top speed. The difference in times between the Speedtail and the company's blisteringly quick P1 is revealing: The P1 takes 15.5 seconds to hit 186mph (top tier numbers by any standard), yet the Speedtail is almost a full four seconds quicker to attain the same speed.

McLaren's future seems secure, which is no small accomplishment in the hypercar space as smaller and newer companies innovate and encroach on the turf of established manufacturers. This is a critical time in the automotive world as the eventual switch to electrification has an uncertain timeline. Some companies were initially caught flat-footed during this transition. Yet now it seems that the rush to eliminate internal combustion engines has been put on hold. McLaren has the fortune of being both successful enough to continue funding development, but small enough that it can switch directions easily. If it continues to anticipate and make the proper adjustments, its future is bright.

McLaren
W1

McLaren's W1 is the new representative of the top rung for the company's street cars. The official successor to their F1 and P1 hypercars, the W1 has a hybrid drivetrain (improved with more power from both the electric and gas motors), and a new carbon fiber monocoque that is lighter and stronger than its predecessors.

The gasoline engine alone, a refinement of the company's 4.0 liter twin turbo V8, is impressive. But with power sitting at 916hp, a car weighing only 3,084 pounds would be plenty quick even for a hypercar. Add in the radial flux electric motor packing 342hp all by itself, and providing instant power the way only electric powerplants can, and the W1 promises to be fast in any situation, from flat out to coming out of a tight corner.

For those twisting tarmac situations, the suspension has notable improvements as well. McLaren's linked hydraulic suspension already sets the standard for comfort and control. This iteration has been improved with more sophisticated cross linking to all four corners. Pitch and dive are precisely managed to keep every tire planted. The suspension modes also adjust active aero to assist with grip where it's needed, and those changes add up at speed—a good thing when over 1,200hp is in play!

Having the top speed electronically limited to 220mph seems almost unfair in a hypercar this capable, but as the W1 is just coming to market, it's safe to assume there will be some room for "improvement" down the road, at least in terms of pure numbers. It's also safe to assume the W1 will still be impressive even by hypercar standards for whoever is lucky enough to experience it.

Acceleration: 0–60mph 2.7 seconds

Torque: 988 lb-ft combined

Power output: 1,258hp combined

Production years: 2025

Production numbers: limited to 399

Engine: 4.0 liter twin turbo V8; 1 radial flux electric

Weight: 3,084 lbs

Price: USD $2,100,000

For the reveal of the W1, McLaren went with an interior in the company's signature orange. Their latest hypercar actually features a smaller center screen, with an emphasis on physical switches and knobs. This reflects a trend among hypercar manufacturers: reduce the presence of capacitive touch screens in favor of more traditional tactile options.

MCLAREN AUTOMOTIVE

Often a car company's attempt to connect its motorsports victories to its street cars is something of a reach. The technology involved in a NASCAR vehicle has little to do with what's available in the showroom beyond the badge. This isn't true with McLaren. Much of what they learn in Formula 1 has been applied directly to cars like the W1. The connected tech between the suspension and the active aero is directly applied knowledge concerning tire grip. Braking hard means weight pitching forward even with stiff suspensions, especially on the street. Having all four shocks lined hydraulically means you can literally push against that pitch and give the rear tires more weight to find grip with.

Adding in a rear wing pitching up not only increases drag but pushes the rear down with aero force, which is a net positive. But then having the computer power to make micrometer-precise adjustments as the car adjusts means it's almost impossible to catch the car off guard since it can adjust and respond in fractions of a second. All that ability to control those commands is incredible, but the computers are only as smart as the people programming them. For that programming, having data pulled directly from Formula 1 races is a substantial advantage.

Mercedes
AMG ONE

Win on Sunday, sell on Monday. That's the old saying used by advertising executives when it came to explaining why manufacturers spent the money and time sponsoring racers and racing teams: Wins translate to conquests on the dealer's sales floor.

At the hypercar level, the connection tends to be more direct. McLaren, Porsche, and Ferrari all boast production cars that have technology derived directly from their competition efforts. That's not surprising for hypercars competing to find every speed advantage. But then, even with the experience some manufacturers have with Formula 1 and Le Mans prototype racing, none of them would be crazy enough to put those engines in a street hypercar.

They left that to sane, sensible Mercedes-Benz.

In a surprise move, Mercedes created the AMG ONE, a hypercar that is powered by both electric motors and the diminutive 1.6 liter turbo V6—also found in the AMG-Petronas Formula 1 racing car. The engine was slightly detuned and strengthened to withstand the rigors of street life.

The model represents a significant achievement. The release of the AMG ONE was delayed as the engineers continued to tweak and refine the drivetrain, making sure it was suitable for a life off the track. But in many ways, suitably, the ONE has been very minimally modified. Its chassis and body panels are fully carbon fiber, and the drivetrain employs three additional electric motors. Inside, the carbon fiber tub features racing bucket seats that are non-adjustable, with both the pedals and steering wheel adjustable for reach instead. The lack of sound deadening material inside means it feels like a race car—because it essentially is one.

Acceleration: 0–60 mpg 2.9 seconds

Power output: 1,049hp combined

Production years: 2024

Production numbers: 275

Engine: 1.6 liter turbocharged V6; 3 electric AC motors

Weight: 3,700 lbs

Price: USD $2,750,000

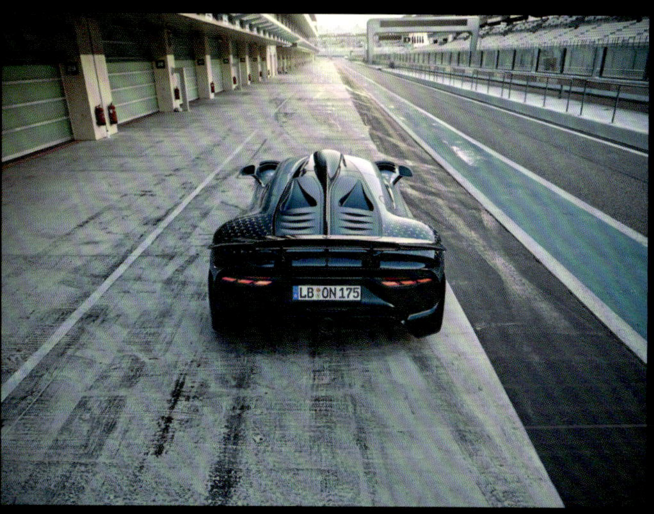

LB ON 175

Mercedes felt no need to pretend this is anything but a repurposed race car. The Mercedes DNA is still present, featuring two tablet screens like many of their production cars, but it otherwise avoids any luxury pretense—including noise reduction or soft-touch surfaces.

MERCEDES AUTOMOTIVE

As wild as the AMG ONE is, the normally staid parent company Mercedes-Benz Group is known for its commitment to serious engineering. Being the oldest existing automobile company gives it a historical relevance than even companies like Ferrari and Porsche can't match.

One enjoyable aspect of observing the German automotive industry is discovering just how intensely competitive companies are with each other. As each new model comes out, you can practically see them sliding around the Nürburgring with grim determination, testing their latest engineering marvels past their limits for proof of concept—in plain view of their competitors.

Even Mercedes has quietly acknowledged that this was a difficult project. One can't predict the future, but the AMG ONE should be celebrated, because another such attempt from any F1 manufacturer is unlikely.

Nio EP9

Acceleration: 0–60mph 2.7 seconds

Torque: 1,092 lbs-ft

Power output: 1,360hp

Production years: 2016–2019

Production numbers: 80

Engine: 4 electric motors, hub-mounted

Weight: 3,825 lbs

Price: USD $1,400,000

With all the great hypercars coming from some of our favorite manufacturers, Chinese manufacturers can be somewhat off the radar. The discussion normally revolves around their more affordable cars in the small sedan and SUV segments. So it's understandable that, given the lack of coverage in western media, enthusiasts might overlook or be completely unaware of the existence of hypercars like the Nio EP9. While production has been slow to ramp up, and most Chinese hypercars are manufactured for their domestic market, things are changing.

While Nio is a Chinese automaker, the EP9 was engineered and built for Nio by RML Automotive, a British company with an extensive motorsports engineering background.

They constructed a chassis built to Le Mans racing prototype standards, and used four hub-mounted motors to create an electric hypercar that was as quick as anything available in the world in 2016. For a car from the previous decade, those specs are still impressive: 1,360hp, 265 miles of electric range, and a top speed of 195mph.

Compared to a Rimac Nevera or a Lotus Evija, the Nio isn't as fast. But the Nio is contextually relevant because it proved that the electric hypercar was not only possible, but possibly capable of beating anything else in the segment with proper development. So, not only is it important in its own right, but the next iteration of this EP9 may well be worth looking out for.

Nio managed to successfully stand out with its first hypercar design. Raised fender lines over the wheels give the exterior great visual drama, while the pronounced splits along the sides that extend and fall down to the leading edge of the rear wheel openings are unique, giving it real presence.

NIO AUTOMOTIVE

Though a young company, Nio has been a notable player in China's electric car manufacturing business. Based in Shanghai, their products are well liked, sell well, and are notable for promoting infrastructure development for electric transportation.

Taking a page from Tesla's success, Nio has been focusing on making it easier to charge their cars when away from home. Their biggest contribution has been the modular construction of their battery packs, making them easy to swap out of cars. They have also been building "swap" stations in China so that owners can access full battery packs while out on the road. To date, there are now about 1,300 of these swap stations operating in China. This concept has been discussed at length in the United States. It would certainly benefit electric car owners. At this point, there are no swap stations in this country. Nor, for that matter, are there any electric models in this country that could take advantage of such infrastructure. Will that change in the future?

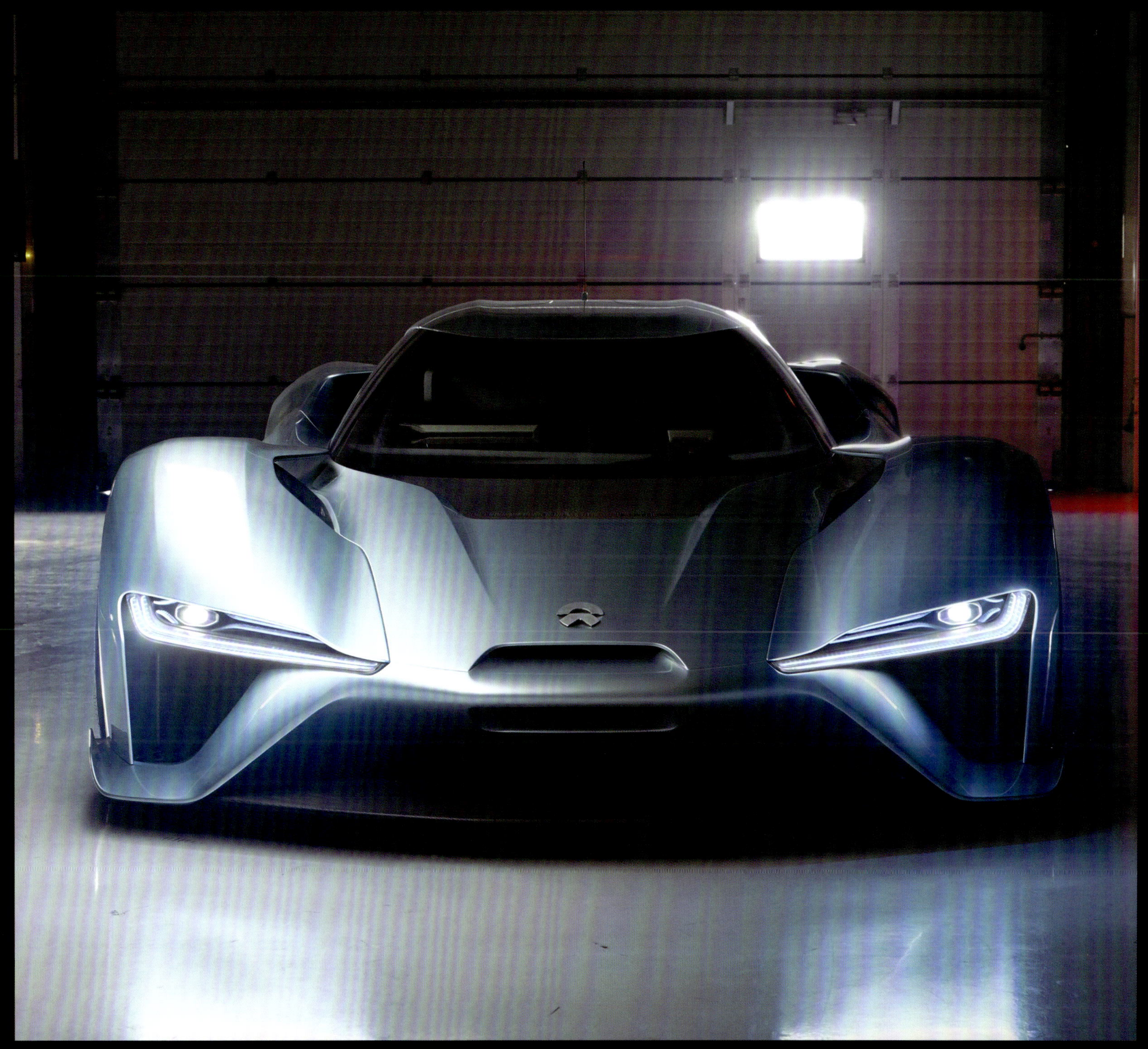

NIO EP9

Noble M600

As impressive as the big manufacturers can be with their premium cars, it's even more impressive when the small companies find a way to compete fair and square on a fraction of the budget. Noble has spent the entirety of its 25-year existence specializing in finding a way to make machines where the whole was greater than the sum of its parts. The company didn't have the funds or inclination to offer complex electronic stability control systems, but instead focused on making their hypercars naturally balanced. So, while its drivetrains, body construction materials and techniques have varied widely, its layouts have remained predictable, featuring a mid engine, rear-wheel drive, and a weight biased slightly to the rear to allow for grip while relying on driver ability to find balance and limits.

The M600 was a built-to-order hypercar available in three body configurations (fiberglass coupe body, carbon fiber coupe body, and carbon fiber targa top). After choosing the body configuration, customers picked from three levels of tuning available for the twin turbo V8 engine used in . . . Volvos. While a seemingly unlikely place to source an engine for a hypercar, Volvo was actually a clever choice by Noble. The motor was very special. It was designed by Yamaha and featured a dynamic and stoutly built 4.4 liter V8, with the top spec producing 650hp. This proved perfectly effective for moving the M600, which weighed in at a lean 2,760 pounds. Contemporary reviews praised the powerful yet progressive nature of the car, noting its proper tuning and balance despite the lack of electronic safety systems.

Acceleration: 0–60mph 3.0 seconds

Torque: 604 lbs-ft

Power output: 650hp

Production years: 2010–2018

Production numbers: 80

Engine: 4.4 liter twin turbo V8

Weight: 2,760 lbs

Noble has always been a small manufacturer competing with giants. While it hews to old school methods, its results seem anything but. Carbon fiber center console details emphasize the serious intent of the M600, and leather-lined carbon buckets are light and supportive. The manual hand brake is a definite throwback in the modern era.

NOBLE AUTOMOTIVE

Noble Automotive was the passion project of Lee Noble, chief designer and engineer as well as part owner of the business bearing his name. The company began operations in 1999. But while he found success early, he wound up selling his interest in the company in 2006, leaving it completely in 2008. The company continued developing and selling its hypercars to the public, even as management came and went. Such a tumultuous existence is a regular occurrence for smaller automotive companies. Noble has managed to endure (though perhaps not flourish), with well-timed improvements and updates keeping it in business. Like all of the smaller manufacturers in this segment, a higher public profile would do this deserving company a lot of good.

Pagani
Huayra

As automotive jewelry goes, nobody does the details like Pagani. With their signature small quad projector headlights standing proudly atop the fenders to the gorgeous interior trim featuring metal switches, toggles, exposed hinge pedals, and gunsight air vents, the Pagani design style is unique and eye-catching. What becomes clear about the Huayra is that it is the product of its creator, Horace Pagani, a designer with a very clear and specific idea of what his cars should be.

With the Huayra, Pagani improved upon its debut model, the Zonda, in both looks and speed, while retaining the design language that had a loyal following. The engine for the Huayra is a variation of a Pagani favorite: the glorious, howling, 6.0 liter V12, sourced from Mercedes-Benz. But in the Pagani, thanks to a well-tuned exhaust, it emits one of the best multi-octave musical sounds in the business. Numbers-wise, a 730hp vehicle weighing less than 3,000 pounds means the Huayra is properly rapid.

The exterior design is familiar, but uses appropriately exotic materials. Pagani employs carbon titanium (or, "carbotanium") in the monocoque. Pagani's background in composites shows up here—he isn't afraid to be the first to utilize high tech materials in his cars.

But the greatness lies in the cohesion of the entire Huayra package. Exterior design, interior detail, and a powerful musical engine paired to a single clutch sequential transmission add up to high entertainment. The Huayra is an event, earning hypercar status in every way.

Acceleration: 0–60mph 2.7 seconds

Torque: 738 lb-ft

Power output: 730hp

Production years: 2011–2018

Production numbers: limited to 100

Engine: 6.0 liter twin turbo V12

Weight: 2,976 lbs

Price: USD $2,400,000

The dual-bubble headlight style was instantly iconic, making the car easily identifiable to hypercar enthusiasts. The cab-forward silhouette is another detail that gives these cars such a unique profile. With the extended rear deck making room for the engine and drivetrain, the cockpit location is suitably aggressive.

PAGANI AUTOMOTIVE

Horace Pagani came to build his own supercar through inspiration. Born in Argentina, he moved to Italy to pursue work as an engineer and designer. Working with Lamborghini starting in the late '80s, he became head of composites development and worked to improve existing Lamborghini models. A solid track record led to his being entrusted with designing new aero body additions for the Countach. New responsibilities included access to a wind tunnel, and this in turn helped him with his personal hypercar projects.

What seems to set Pagani apart is not only his intelligence, but his genuine enthusiasm for fast cars. While he has established a wizardly reputation for creating cars from the ground up, he has also shown a generous enthusiasm for Ferrari and Porsche. He freely admits to both driving those makes and owning a few. For all his admiration for other manufacturers, however, his vision for his own hypercars is clear and distinct.

Pagani Utopia

The Utopia is Pagani's latest and greatest hypercar. Presented in 2022, it was a step up in power and pace from the Huayra it replaced. But as with all Pagani products, the details are where the Utopia shines.

Not just a reskinned Huayra, the Utopia features an all-new carbon titanium chassis with carbon fiber sections that is lighter and stronger than its predecessors. Its Mercedes-Benz V12 was retuned to produce 852hp. Slicker aerodynamics have boosted performance too.

As the Utopia doesn't add either hybrid power or all-wheel drive, Pagani made it clear that the Utopia is committed to the old-school approach to a hypercar. It is driver oriented and simplified. To that end, Pagani leaned into its own mandate by bringing back the manual transmission option—true three pedal, shift it yourself manual transmissions, along with the single clutch automated transmission in case owners wanted their hypercar to take care of the shifting for them.

Inside, Pagani's nod to current gauge panel layouts is a single lone screen, nestled between the analog rpm counter and speedometer in the drivers binnacle. Other than that, there's metal switchgear, toggles, and four backlit analog gauges in the center. Pagani believes this approach is more timeless and individualistic compared to the tendency towards screen proliferation and quickly-dated digital components. The Utopia accentuates its throwback looks with lovely round knobs with detents for the climate controls. The result is pleasingly tactile and solid.

At some point in the future, the company will have to incorporate electric motors of some kind to meet tightening regulations all over the world. But Horace Pagani's market niche is solid. Loyal Pagani customers don't really want him to make electric hypercars simply because they aren't as fun or engaging. Whatever the future solution may be, Pagani can be expected to forge a smart and elegant one.

Acceleration: 0–60 2.9 seconds

Torque: 811 lb-ft

Power output: 852hp

Production years: starting in 2023

Production numbers: 99

Engine: 6.0 liter twin turbo V12

Weight: 2,822 lbs

Price: USD $2,250,000

The Utopia boasts the usual fantastic attention to detail that Pagani brings to its designs. The interior switchgear in particular has a solid-hewn look, with the big rotary knobs and dials Pagani has always been known for.

PAGANI AUTOMOTIVE

Pagani has created another winner, and once again his interior design deserves special mention. The Utopia, like its two predecessors, benefits from the special attention paid to switchgear and mechanical connections. From the solid click metal buttons to the exposed hinges on the pedals in the footwell, this hypercar does not attempt to isolate occupants from the experience. That would miss the point.

To that end, the Utopia line now includes a Roadster version as well. It sports a clear removable roof which adds a little festive drama to the ride. As is normal for Pagani products, all production models of the Utopia are spoken for. However, Pagani has been known to relent and make extra examples of a discontinued model because his rabidly loyal customers ask repeatedly!

Pagani Zonda

The Pagani Zonda was the company's first model, yet nothing about it looked or felt like a first effort. The Zonda's detail and execution far exceeded the quality standards of most smaller companies. This quality was informed by Horacio Pagani's experience at Lamborghini as head of the composites department.

With his ability to build his own platform established, Pagani needed to find an existing engine. Enter Mercedes-Benz. He secured an agreement to purchase the V12 already in production for their S-class sedan and SL Roadster. It was a compact, relatively light powerplant.

Coupled with a six-speed manual transmission, the first Zondas were equipped with the relatively tame 6.0 liter version of the V12 and put out 389hp, making them quick enough, but also revealing that the platform could handle substantially more. Pagani began working with Mercedes to use substantially larger engines. After less than two years in production the Zonda S arrived, with a 7.0 liter engine and 542hp, making for a huge improvement in speed. Yet only a year after that, the Zonda 7.3 S arrived. This model boasted a 7.3 liter version, strengthened pistons and crankshaft, and other improvements to key moving parts, resulting in 547hp, not a huge jump in total power, but more power at lower revs for more flexibility.

Although the Huayra essentially replaced the Zonda in 2011, Pagani would build special versions for his customers until 2019. Considering that this equated to two full decades of production, the Zonda may hold the record for longest hypercar production on one chassis.

Production years: 1999–2019

Engine: 6.0 liter V12, 7.3 liter V12

Weight: 2,822 lbs

PAGANI AUTOMOTIVE

The Zonda set a standard for the Pagani company. It was a hypercar particularly focused on not just outright speed, but also full driver involvement. When Horace Pagani first began developing his hypercar, it was originally going to be named after one of Pagani's friends from his native Argentina, the Formula 1 racing legend Juan Manuel Fangio. Its working name was "Fangio F1." But when Fangio died in 1995, Pagani changed the name to Zonda (a Spanish word for the hot summer wind in Argentina).

The Mercedes V12 was critical to the Zonda's initial success, and its continual upgrades and improvements kept it relevant. The initial 389hp version was solid, but the increase in displacement made huge differences. And soon Mercedes and Zonda moved to twin turbocharging. Pagani tailored its products to continual power increases, keeping pace with this trend in the market. Pagani will never try to be a high volume manufacturer, but it will continue to set the standard for detail and quality for its loyal customers.

The original Pagani hypercar set the standard for interior design appointments. Air vents set into polished steel nacelles sit proudly above the stereo, and an exposed instrumentation pod with no hood emphasizes the Zonda's mechanical nature.

Pininfarina B95

Acceleration: 0–60mph 2.0 seconds

Power output: 1,900hp

Production years: 2025

Production numbers: 10

Engine: 4 electric motors, hub mount

Price: USD $4,800,000

With success comes confidence. For Pininfarina, that confidence came from the reaction to their introductory coachworks offering, the Battista. After finding such a welcome audience for its tailored design draped over the chassis of the Rimac Nevera, they realized there was a market for the sort of no-holds-barred designs they had been known for in their heyday.

From that positive energy came the B95 Speedster, with B standing for Barchetta. The B95 once again taps the Nevera electric hypercar platform, only this time the body comes without a windshield, and provides just the barest hint of wind deflection. The leather bucket seats are framed by rollover hoops/humps extending back down to the rear of the B95, matching well with the signature rising curve on top of the fenders. With front and rear splitters for airflow management, the B95 still incorporates Pininfarina design cues: there's a sharp-edged nose and a full air intake at the trailing edge of the hood to aid downforce. The look is suitably dramatic, but the overall shape, even with all the sharp-lined aero aids, is classic Pininfarina.

While acceleration is every bit as intense, the top speed cap of 185 is most likely the result of a decision to minimize just how much air occupants had to deal with!

Bespoke interior options really stand out when there's no roof or windshield to hide them. The detail in this example draws the eye, with its optional checkered cloth headrest and upper wings. It pairs nicely with the supple brown leather-lined interior below the cowl line.

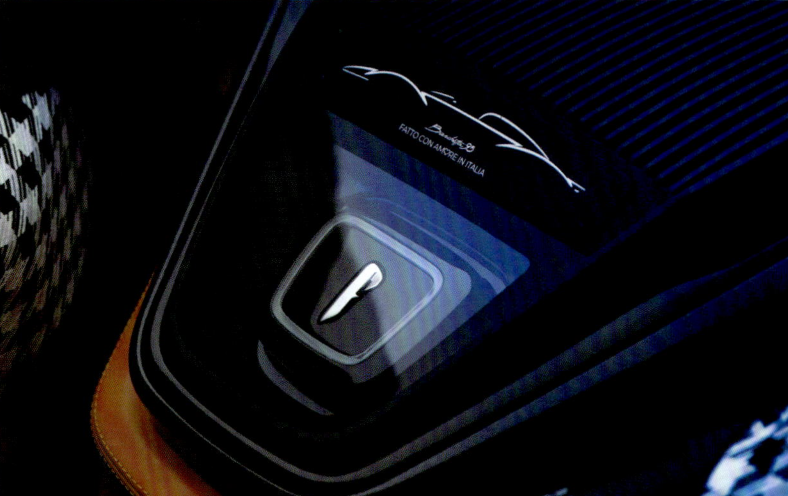

PININFARINA AUTOMOTIVE

Once Pininfarina saw success with the Battista, they were inspired by the possibilities. The malleability of the hardware meant they could use computer-aided design and 3D printing to conjure a new working prototype in a short amount of time, and with minimum capital invested. So, with the first project completed, and production lessons learned, the second project could be produced even more quickly and efficiently.

Pininfarina

Battista

The Battista is the first electric hypercar produced by the automotive division of the design house Pininfarina. Named after the founder of the original company, Battista Pininfarina, this 1,900hp hypercar taps into a classic Pininfarina methodology: It takes an existing vehicle, drapes it in gorgeous Italian design, then sells it to the public looking for something rare and beautiful that will stand apart from the crowd.

Pinifarina's partner for this exercise was Rimac, the company responsible for the paradigm-shifting Nevera hypercar. Rimac has been a leader in designing efficient electric power, so much so that legacy manufacturers go to them for help with their electric technology. Their Revera is already known for being so brutally quick that it even leaves Bugatti Chirons dropped behind, and the bodywork is handsome and purposeful, befitting anything capable of 258mph.

But while the Revera looks good, the Battista exterior gets to riff off design cues Pininfarina have been applying for decades to their creations. The rising curves over the wheel wells are reflected by the fenders, and sharp creases in the nose rake forward for airflow and visual drama. The Battista successfully blends modern hypercar downforce design with gentler curves derived from their best 1960s designs. As a partner to Nimac, Battista manages to complement purposeful functionality with truly unique flourish. The best part for both is how easy it is to rearrange the basic chassis to accommodate design language differences and individuality.

Acceleration: 0–60mph 2.0 seconds

Power output: 1,900hp

Production years: 2022

Production numbers: limited to 150

Engine: 4 electric motors, hub mount

Weight: 2,548 lbs

Price: USD $2,200,000

If you've got it, flaunt it. When you have access to Rimac's world-beating electric drivetrain, and you're one of the most legendary automotive design houses in history, you might as well show off. Classic Pininfarina styling in a modern idiom, motivated by 1,900hp, is hard to beat.

PININFARINA AUTOMOTIVE

With the Battista, the Pininfarina was looking both forward and backward by fully embracing its design house roots. The exciting thing about electrification for any manufacturer is the ease with which electric motors can be integrated into vehicles. Their compactness and the variety of choices about where they can be located (under a hood, along the axle, hub mounted, etc.) gives the designers of the platform and exterior free reign to make what they want with minimal concessions to engine space or location. With those constraints eliminated, the purest version of a designer's concept can be realized and put on the market.

Pininfarina has a long history of producing wild concept designs for show cars. The new technological reality means such companies can flourish. Architecture constraints have been loosened, the preproduction development cycle is shorter, and considerations like adequate cooling airflow for the engine are becoming obsolete. For car manufacturers, especially small ones running a tight budget, this makes the path to success much shorter, and more likely.

Porsche
718 Cayman GT4 RS

Acceleration: 0–60mph 2.8 seconds

Torque: 331 lb-ft

Power output: 493hp

Production years: 2022

Engine: 4.0 liter flat six

Weight: 3,242 lbs

Price: USD $168,495

The Cayman GT4 RS is the machine enthusiasts begged Porsche to make for years. While some people opined that the 718 Cayman and 718 Boxster twins were not to be taken seriously, many driving enthusiasts knew the truth: these small, light, two seater sports cars had some tangible advantages over their bigger, iconic GT sibling. The engine layout was inherently more stable, if less entertaining, and the smaller size and weight were an advantage. If Porsche would only give them more power, went the thinking. For the first two decades of their lives, these models always had the options for better suspensions and some more power, but they always had just enough to make them fun, but not enough to threaten the 911's supremacy.

But finally, with the 718 Cayman GT4 RS, Porsche went all-in. A product of Porsche's GT department, it is equipped with the engine from the GT3. That equates to 493hp from a naturally aspirated flat six engine that redlines at 9000 rpm. In the RS version, the intake piping is directly behind the heads of the occupants, getting air from intake ducting mounted where the rear glass would be in the standard GT4. Stiffer suspension and light materials make this not only light but agile in the extreme.

While the GT4 RS is relatively affordable for a hypercar, it's another example of what customers want from their purchases—the opportunity to own a limited production example from their favorite manufacturers. The RS, in particular, allows buyers to select full option packages with carbon fiber body panels, forged magnesium wheels, carbon ceramic brakes, and many other light weight specifications that make a car truly special to its owner.

The key ingredients for the Porsche RS models are all present: center tachometer, alcantara touch points, and engine and suspension mode switches readily at hand. For the Cayman version, the air intakes are placed directly behind the headrests (the better to hear the engine's song at full volume).

PORSCHE AUTOMOTIVE

The history of the smaller Porsches is one of limited success. At first, everything stemmed from the simple 356 platform. But since the 911 replaced the 356, entry level sporting models have come and gone. The 914, 924, 944, and 968 have had their moments in the sun, but they weren't anything like the 911. Sales were decent, but eventually dropped off.

The Boxster/Cayman twins were always a little different, because they were very similar to their big brother 911. Coming out in the late 1990s, the Boxster shared many parts (including much of the nose) with the 911. Their layouts were very similar, the interiors nearly identical, and even the flat six engines have generally been much the same. So, in many important ways, they felt like true Porsches.

Porsche 911 GT3 RS

As Porsche continues to build on its incredible success in the new century, there is one model that provides both a diversity of options and continuity with the past. The street legal track spec 911 has been available since 1964. Of course, what constitutes "track specification" has become significantly more complex and technology-based than it was over 60 years ago. However, the 911 GT3 RS leans into its purpose with typical German seriousness. The GT street car lineup became available in 1999, starting with the first GT3. It was a driver-oriented car that did not set out to be the fastest in the lineup. But that focus on driver enjoyment served it well. It had naturally aspirated engines with manual transmissions, more track-ready suspension tuning that was stiffer than the Grand Touring comfort of their Turbo models, and rear-wheel drive for weight and handling complexity.

As technology progressed, the GT3 RS evolved. The latest GT3 RS no longer offers a manual transmission equipped with three pedals. The dual-clutch PDK transmission not only upshifts faster than any driver ever could but it also downshifts and maintains the right gear thanks to its modern electronic control. Coupled with driver-selected modes for levels of traction control, torque vectoring, suspension stiffness, and drag reduction from the rear wing, the Porsche allows the driver to tailor the car's settings almost infinitely. The level of interaction goes beyond even what some enthusiasts would consider. But if anyone is going to approach the hypercar market with serious intent, it's the engineers at Porsche.

Acceleration: 0–60mph 2.7 seconds

Torque: 342 lb-ft

Power output: 518hp

Production years: 2023

Engine: 4.0 liter flat six engine

Weight: 3,216 lbs

Price: USD $241,300

Porsche's GT3 RS included a big rear wing that was substantially larger and wider than that of the "regular" GT3. The center-lock alloy wheels and front dive planes also stand out on the RS version.

PORSCHE AUTOMOTIVE

The 911's GT3 is certainly the most "involving" version of the 911 line. But thanks to Porsche's diverse goals with this line, buyers can also purchase a more coddling and protecting model: the 911 Turbo. This model represents Porsche's leading edge in the business. It was among the first to introduce turbocharging and the first to incorporate all-wheel drive into sports cars. Porsche successfully got bigger power out of smaller engines and better grip where other setups would struggle for traction. The 911 Turbo was not only fast, but it was also predictable in a way cars without all-wheel drive can't be.

The existence and success of both the GT3 and Turbo models speak to how advanced hypercars have become. The Turbo is so advanced, so capable, and so easy to pilot, that it almost seems to provide too little involvement for some enthusiast drivers. Hence the GT3: Porsche found it necessary to put some excitement back into the car. That included less sound deadening, stiffer suspensions, and rear-drive only to intentionally grip less. Either version is a true hypercar. It's just a question of how you want that hyper speed experience delivered.

Porsche 918 Spyder

At the dawn of the hybrid hypercar era, three choices existed: the Ferrari LaFerrari, the McLaren P1, and the Porsche 918 Spyder. The choices represented three very distinct personalities and approaches to sports cars. Porsche saw their mission a little differently than the other two, as the 918 is the only one to have an electric-only driving capability. In electric mode, it's capable of decently brisk driving speeds and is good for about 12 miles.

While this feature had its advantages, clearly buyers in the hypercar market expect more. So when the 608hp flat V8 engine fires up and joins the party, proper speed is easily attained. With the seven-speed dual clutch PDK transmission, the 918 Spyder has proper race car pace on any racetrack, making it a true Porsche product in every sense. And from a design perspective, it seems like a direct descendant of the incredible Carrera GT, a distinctly analog sports car with a naturally aspirated V10, a manual transmission, and no electronic driver aids. But that car also had a reputation for being tricky to control.

The 918 Spyder has the opposite reputation—all the sound and fury but blessed with excellent traction systems to keep the driver free from a code red situation. This ability to make hypercar speed feel natural and easy for the average enthusiast was an achievement even for Porsche.

Acceleration: 0–60mph 2.6 seconds

Torque: 944 lb-ft

Power output: 887hp combined

Production years: 2013–2015

Engine: 4.6 liter V8, 2 AC electric motors

Weight: 3,700 lbs

Price: USD $848,000

The interior design of the 918 took its influence from its Carrera GT predecessor, minus the earlier hypercar's manual transmission shifter on the rising center console. Even with multiple drive options to select from between the engine and electric power, Porsche has retained a clean and uncluttered interior look.

The 918 Spyder was an incredible accomplishment, yet nobody expected any less from Porsche. Porsche had been on a roll for the whole of the 21st century, so while people were sad to see Porsche stick to their low production totals, they were excited to see what would come next.

People are still waiting. With the success of the GT and Turbo lines, Porsche was kept busy producing special versions of their 911s for hardcore fans. Rumors might fly, but in truth, Porsche hasn't needed to push the envelope or kick out model after model. The existing platforms have flourished. Special versions of not just sports cars, but even models like the Cayenne, have satisfied customer desire. Other manufacturers like Lamborghini, Aston Martin, and Ferrari have taken note. Still, the rumors continue to fly. Sometime in 2025, Porsche will likely rejoin the fray with a potential follow-up to the 918.

Nevera

With an available 1,914 horsepower, the all-electric Rimac Nevera screeched to 60mph from a stop in under two seconds. The product of a Croatian "sports car" maker with ties to Bugatti, the Nevera was first seen at the 2019 Geneva Auto Show. Power for the Nevera's four electric motors was supplied by a 120-kWh lithium-ion battery which provided a claimed 340 miles of driving range. Production of the $2.4 million sports car was limited to 150 vehicles.

Acceleration: 0–60mph 1.9 seconds

Torque: 1,741 lb-ft

Power output: 1,888hp

Production years: 2022

Engine: 4 electric motors, hub mounted

Weight: 4,993 lbs

Price: USD $2,200,000

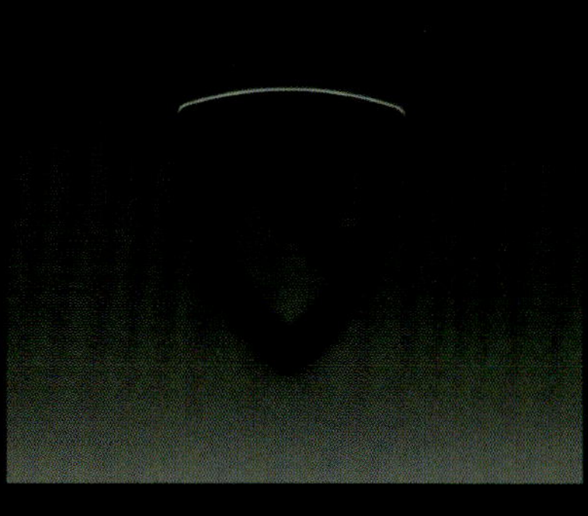

By hypercar standards, the Rimac's sharp exterior design gives little indication of its record-breaking capability. Downforce provided by the large wing and body sculpting are crucial here, but it remains otherwise purposeful and clean.

RIMAC

RIMAC AUTOMOTIVE

All emerging hypercar companies know that getting a foothold in the business isn't just a matter of providing good looks and power. It's also about investment and support. Promising hypercars and companies have come and gone, not because their products weren't worthy, but due to simple business challenges. Angel investors are so-named because they are the answer to a prayer as much as the result of hard work.

The best way to tip the odds in your favor is to be demonstrably better than everyone you compete against. And Rimac technology has proven to be at the forefront of electric car efficiency and power. Proof of this ability lies not in the Nevera itself, but rather in what other companies are impressed by. As of this writing, Rimac is either a technological partner or provider for companies like Porsche, BMW, Hyundai/Kia, and Pininfarina for their electric car platforms. This list of upper-tier companies speaks volumes for the Rimac brand.

SSC

Tuatara

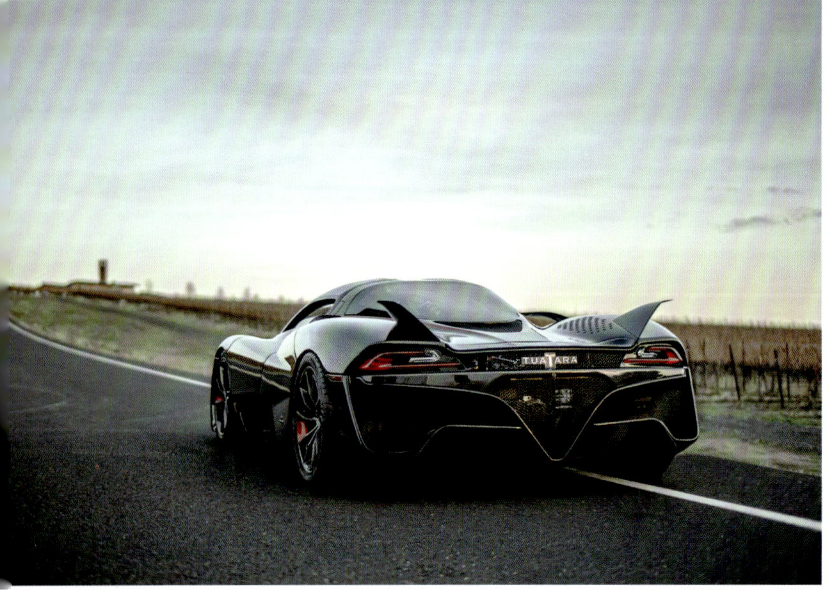

While electric hypercars dominate the landscape, it's easy to overlook good old American V8 horsepower. There are still knowledgeable, hands-on companies that know how to marry techniques from the past and present. They pair modern electronic fueling systems with tried-and-true hot rod engine building using all the time-honored basics paired with micrometer-precise tolerances and fueling to create big, reliable horsepower.

Some people have forgotten, but certainly not SSC North America. They also haven't forgotten that they were in a legitimate fight with Bugatti for the claim to fastest production car in the world. Starting with their first car, the Ultimate Aero, SSC held the Guinness record for fastest car for years.

The Tuatara was truly next-level fast. The engine, built for SSC by Nelson Racing Engines, was originally a 6.5 liter flat-plane crank V8, but for production it was decreased to 5.9 liters to allow a higher redline without the reciprocating parts flying apart. In its most powerful form, it held the two-way average speed record of 282.9mph. Unlike its Bugatti competitor, it was not equipped with stability controls, traction aids, or any electronic safety net. It was a rear-wheel drive car that needed a good driver to achieve its speed. One could not just turn on all the proper systems, aim for the horizon, and hold on.

SSC has developed a few variations of the Tuatara that include a track-focused Striker. This model is kitted with additional downforce that lowers top speed but greatly increases grip. The Aggressor, which is not street legal, is stripped of luxury features and tuned to produce 2,200hp.

Acceleration: 0–60mph 2.5 seconds

Power output: 1,350–2,200hp

Production years: 2020–present

Production numbers: 100 planned

Engine: 5.9 liter twin turbo V8

Weight: 2,750 lbs

Price: USD $1,600,000

The exterior of the Tuatara not only manages high speed stability, but also engine cooling. In contrast to electric hypercars, the Tuatara's exterior features multiple intakes located at the front, sides, and on top of the back deck to ensure the considerable engine heat is dissipated quickly and efficiently.

SHELBY SUPERCARS AUTOMOTIVE

Jerod Shelby, the founder of SSC North America, has stayed true to the solo proprietor ethic. The continued world record achievements of his hypercars give his company the attention needed to succeed, but even by his own admission, those top speed records can make his cars seem like one-trick ponies. This can overshadow their well-rounded abilities. Neither the Tuatara or the Ultimate Aero were straight line drag cars. They were balanced driver's cars meant for the track or twisty road work, enhanced by the impressive power that the engines produced.

That approach informs the decision to have two different track-focused versions of the Tuatara. The approach fits the expectations of the hypercar market, where cars are always fast in a straight line, but are also top tier in all relevant categories. That said, at this point, making hypercars without any electric assistance, and sticking to gasoline engines running rear-wheel drive only, is now officially a minority choice.

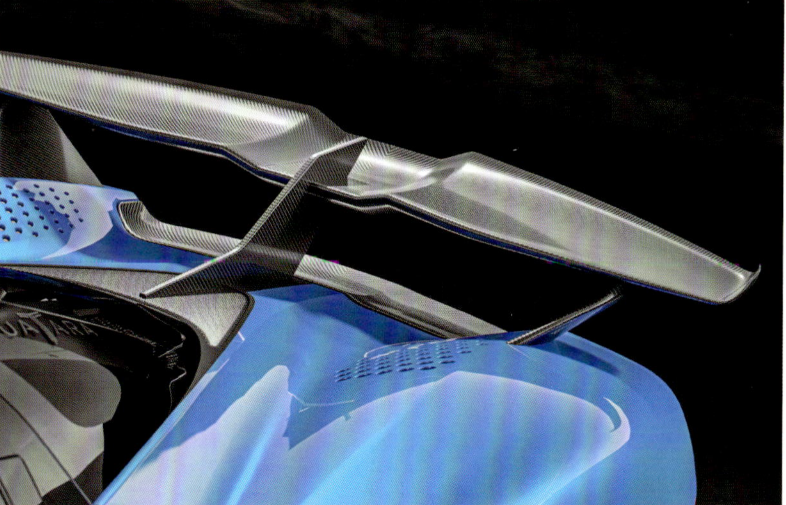

Ultima RS

Ultima was founded by the dedicated hypercar maven Lee Noble, the man who is also responsible for . . . Noble. These companies overlap both chronologically and philosophically. They make powerful mid-engine rear-wheel drive coupes with great handling balance and big power delivered without electronic intervention.

Ultima is a British company. Its tube frame road-legal RS is a hypercar that relies on Lee Noble's extensive experience in making balanced and capable track machines with a wide range of Chevrolet V8s. Options start with a 430hp aspirated V8, a 6.4 liter supercharged option with 650hp, and extend to the hypercar spec: a 6.5 liter with a larger supercharger that starts at 800hp which can be tuned to produce the full 1,200hp.

Here's the thing (in the U.S. anyway) about that "road-legal" part. For the Ultima to be considered legal, it has to be built by the owner from a kit. The kit requires no outside parts. In fact, only supplied parts may be used. This is how Ultima circumvents the tedious and expensive certification test that every new car must pass in order to be sold in the United States. For some potential owners, this aspect is a disqualifying one. But for many enthusiasts this is a valued part of the experience.

Acceleration: 0–60mph 2.5 seconds

Power output: 1,200hp

Production years: 2019

Engine: 6.4 liter supercharged V8

Weight: 2,050 lbs

Price: USD $120,000

For fans of traditional internal combustion engines, the Ultima RS's open clamshell properly shows off the Chevrolet-based V8 powerplant. It is a supercharged wonder, utilizing relatively mild upgrades to achieve an impressive 1,200-plus hp.

ULTIMA AUTOMOTIVE

Imagine starting a hypercar company and parting ways with it to make the same kind of hypercar. That was Lee Noble's situation. Lee Noble started his namesake company and made it functional and productive. But it took the Marlow family (who started as customers and wound up buying the company) to improve the company's business side of the equation. During this time, Lee Noble learned from the growing pains of his first company, and now heads Ultima.

It's the perfect example of not taking business decisions too personally. Noble and Ultima's state of coexistence is a win for everyone. Both manufacturers continue to do well even as they take different approaches to marketing and selling their very similar hypercars. Regardless of how the companies got to this point, their hypercars are special for both their ability and their relatively low asking prices, making them accessible for enthusiasts in a way something like the Bugatti or Ferrari hybrid hypercars could never be.

W Motors

Fenyr SuperSport

If the Lykan HyperSport allowed W Motors to walk, then the Fenyr SuperSport is what allows it to run. As the second model from the Dubai-based hypercar company, the Fenyr SuperSport is a refined product in every way, from design details and specifications to the methods of manufacturing and production that allow better economies of scale. While the company also plans to have SUVs for production in the future, the hypercar segment is their natural home.

As with the original model, any details beyond the specifications of the Fenyr SuperSport were initially scarce. We now know that the company has refined its production methods, and this model has proven to be just as quick as the Lykan. Its list price of only USD $1.9 million reflects the company's improved efficiency.

The engine is the same Ruf-sourced twin turbocharged flat six, putting out 799hp to the rear wheels, slightly more than the Lykan. It's clear that the Fenyr is no little brother to the Lykan. It is a more refined and quicker model all around.

Acceleration: 0–60mph 2.8 seconds

Torque: 723 lb-ft

Power output: 799hp

Production years: 2019

Production numbers: est. 100

Engine: 3.8 liter twin turbo flat six engine

Weight: 3,120 lbs

Price: USD $1,900,000

The Fenyr SuperSport's angular lines are highlighted by the rising curves above the wheels that lay over a tight and muscular shape. The Ruf-derived, twin turbocharged flat six benefits from proper air intakes that are well hidden along the sides, keeping an emphasis on the compact size of this Dubai hypercar.

W MOTORS AUTOMOTIVE

The W Motors story is informed by a simple truth in business—go where the money is. Founded in 2012 in Lebanon, the company first consisted of a like-minded Lebanese and Italian group. Having corporate offices in Dubai is smart not only for access to potential investors, but also for being based in a culture that is among the most passionate in the hypercar community. Car enthusiasts in Dubai are very proud of the fact that this is a hypercar company from their country. Tapping that sense of pride becomes another source of inspiration for the company.

Dubai in particular has seen incredible growth in the last 20 years, both financially and in total population. That growth is likely to continue. In every aspect, the locale of the company should allow them to expand and grow. This hopefully means seeing more exciting projects from them in the future.

W Motors
Lykan HyperSport

The Lykan HyperSport was the first hypercar (in fact, the first product) manufactured by newcomer W Motors. As a first effort, it managed to pull of an impressive technical achievement, matching an engine from a legendary tuner to exceptional design details created with the home market in mind. The Lykan suffered somewhat from a lack of press coverage due to the company's location. This resulted in some dismissive skepticism about the company—and even the model's existence. But W has proven the doubters wrong. While only seven examples of the Lykan HyperSport exist, the owners (including the Dubai police) have been seen in public enjoying the cars.

The design team started with a flat six-cylinder twin turbocharged engine producing 740hp. For anyone that knows their engine configurations, a flat six engine immediately narrows the possible sources for it, and sure enough, it comes from Alois Ruf and his legendary Porsche tuning company. The engine is mounted in the mid-rear of the car. It uses Porsche's dual clutch PDK transmission to drive the rear wheels. The engine's location helps the model achieve grip under power.

The shape is properly aero-friendly. While details about the model are scarce, one design element has received a lot of attention: The headlights incorporate diamonds. The company offers customers the option of embedded jewels in the design, and these also include rubies and sapphires.

While details about the Lykan HyperSport are scant, its existence has allowed the company to continue to grow. The model served as the basis for the subsequent Fenyr SuperSport.

Acceleration: 0–60mph 2.8 seconds

Torque: 708 lb-ft

Power output: 740hp

Production years: 2014–2018

Production numbers: 7

Engine: 3.7 liter twin turbocharged flat six engine

Weight: 3,042 lbs

Price: USD $3,400,000

W MOTORS AUTOMOTIVE

The first product for W Motors was well received. They had managed all the difficulties involved in getting their product to market. But while the product was a success, the purchase price was substantial, even by hypercar standards. Of course, since the company was based in the UAE, this wasn't an insurmountable obstacle. More importantly, the price wasn't an example of greed. Bringing an all-new car to market for the first time takes a lot of work and substantial investment. But the second model from W Motors had a much lower price. This was the result of simply refining what had already proven to be viable and not having to start from scratch. In short, economies of scale are all relative, and sticking to a great idea and following through has its rewards.

Zenvo

Aurora

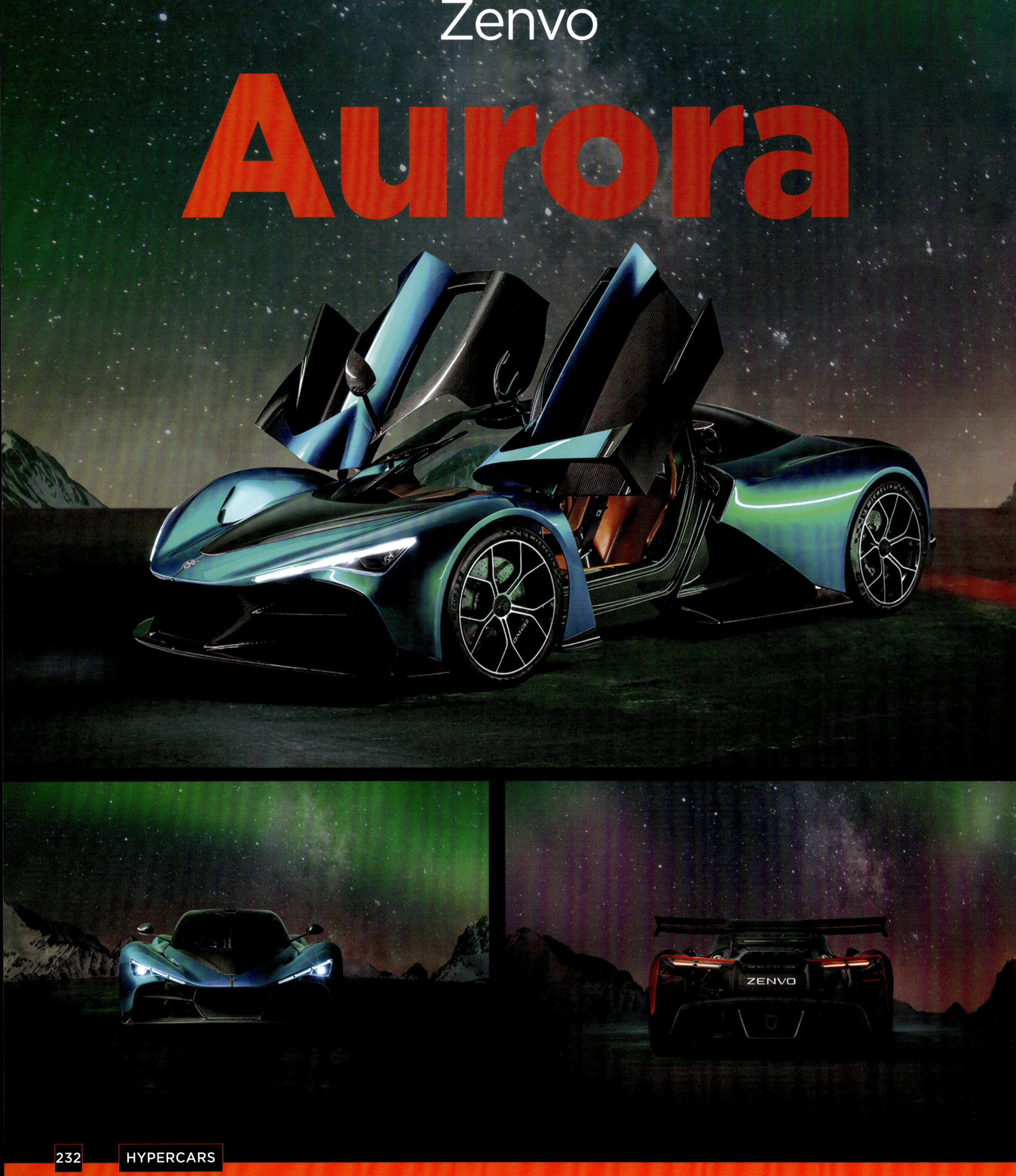

With the Aurora line, Zenvo ambitiously set out to expand their capabilities and point towards the future with their first hybrid platform. They were no longer content to rely on gradual progress. The previous Zenvos relied on GM-based V8 architecture with added twin superchargers and some intelligent redesigns of the internals to create modified engines that minimized expense.

With the Aurora, Zenvo has clearly decided to swing hard. The combustion engine is a quad-turbocharged V12, the first used by the company. In addition, the V12 mill is augmented by two AC electric motors. This results in a hypercar-appropriate output at a combined 1,850 horsepower. In another first, the Aurora will have available all-wheel drive as an option. Buyers will also have the choice of rear-wheel drive for added thrill. The more aggressive sport option is designated the Aurora Agil. It features more aero, stiffer suspension specs, and the rear-drive configuration. The more relaxed touring-oriented option is the Aurora Tur. It goes with all-wheel drive and a more luxurious specification.

Zenvo is still sticking to low production totals with its Auroras. Only 100 will be built (split exactly 50/50 between the two). What remains to be seen is which version of the Aurora will be more popular with buyers as well as what they plan to use them for: track day toy or rolling street art? Production begins in 2025. The Auroras are all-new and represent a logical progression for the Danish company as they look to make a bigger impact on the hypercar landscape.

Acceleration: 0–60mph 2.3 seconds

Power output: 1,850hp combined

Production years: est. 2025

Production numbers: est. 100

Engine: 6.6 liter quad-turbo V12, two AC electric motors

Weight: 3,197 lbs

Price: USD $2,800,000

The Aurora isn't the first hypercar to utilize butterfly doors for entry. But Zenvo's doors extend not only into the roof, but also down and below the entry sill. Access is not only easy, but also shows off the interior and carbon tub to great effect.

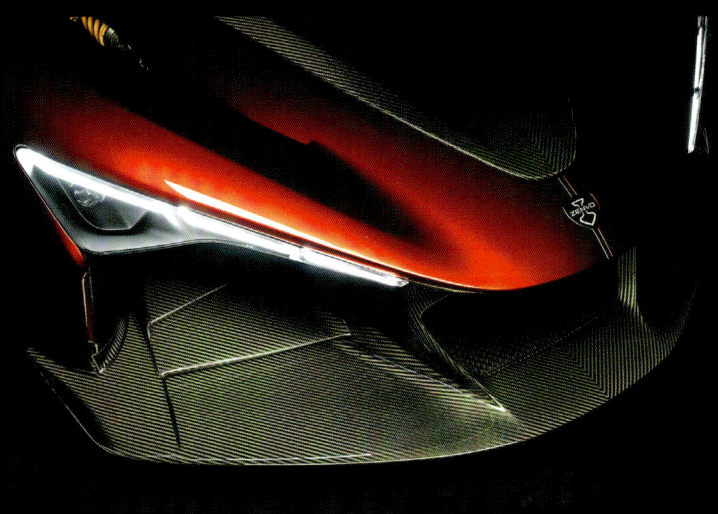

ZENVO AUTOMOTIVE

For a small two-man operation out of a country not known for cars, Zenvo has managed to draw attention to itself effectively. Nestled in a small town an hour south of Copenhagen, the company slowly but surely put together a succession of refined small-batch hypercars. They may not be well known, but their efforts have made headway.

But that headway doesn't guarantee success. As with all companies at this level, it often takes a little outside help to get that extra push to success. Zenvo is no different. With reported help from an investor group out of Prague, the company continues to focus on the hypercar market exclusively.

That focus can be called dedication, but interviews with the founders make it sound almost accidental. The engineer of the two, Troels Vollertsen, says that creating a hypercar wasn't their intention at the beginning—it just wound up that way as their work progressed. The implication of that statement is that the process was organic and not a result of a target. It's a remarkable approach to hypercar production, and it seems counterintuitive. Consider that the creation of a car like the Bugatti Veyron was the result of an engineering team being told to hit performance targets that seemed almost impossible—quite the opposite of an artist's approach. But there's always more than one path to success.

Zenvo

TSR-GT

The TSR-GT is the relatively relaxed version of the TSR platform. The TSR is a dedicated track version of the platform, weighing over 500 pounds less than this GT specification, with no sound deadening, a roll cage and race bucket seats with full six-point racing harnesses, and an engine tuned for more power delivered at the higher engine speeds normally experienced in a track car.

The appropriately designated GT spec has a less extreme cabin and tuning. Its aero management is notably less dramatic, with a smaller, fixed rear wing. Inside the cabin, the addition of leather upholstery and trim instead of bare carbon makes the interior quieter and more inviting, though no less serious in its mission.

But don't mistake its more comfortable mission to mean less speed. With the smaller wing comes better aerodynamics. In fact, this actually increases the power of the twin supercharged V8 to 1,360hp. Along with the less aggressive bodywork, aerodiscs on the front wheels smooth the airflow down the side of the GT, reducing drag. These changes give a higher top speed for the GT (a manufacturer-claimed 263mph). That's significantly more than the drag- and gear-limited 202mph of the other TSRs. It's a dramatic difference, but given the power that these hypercars have, it speaks more to the effectiveness of the downforce and gearing on the other variations than any lack of power. For a touring hypercar, having the potential to access big speeds when traveling through multiple countries in Europe is a serious mission statement.

Acceleration: 0–60mph 2.8 seconds

Torque: 811 lb-ft

Power output: 1,360hp

Production years: 2016–2019

Production numbers: 15

Engine: 5.8 liter twin supercharged V8

Weight: 2,932 lbs

Price: USD $1,800,000

The interior is clean and features plenty of carbon fiber. But, bucking the recent trend towards matte interior finishes, the TSR-S features a glossy finish for the carbon pieces and has an overall sophisticated and polished look that brings substance to the trim.

ZENVO AUTOMOTIVE

Zenvo Automotive was formed in Denmark in 2007 by Jesper Jensen and Troels Vollertsen. Originally named the Nordic Sports Car A/S, it was focused from the beginning on producing a hypercar. Within two years, they had created their first product, the ST1. This model used a Chevrolet LS7 V8 as a base, but was enhanced with the twin supercharger setup they've used for most of their models since then. While they only made 15 examples of that car, the short window from concept to production release was remarkable. An STI appearance with Jay Leno helped raise awareness of their existence—a critical bit of publicity that helped their survival.

Despite their boutique size and the relative obscurity that comes from being based in northern Europe, Zenvo has managed to move forward and develop new models consistently. They have continued to focus on developing new engines based on Chevrolet V8's, but also continue to make substantial changes, whether flat-plane cranks, twin supercharger integration, or via continued testing and development.

McLaren
SENNA
MN MC 1

AM10:00~PM7:30
チュア無線本館